WHERE I STAND

ALSO BY THE AUTHOR

Suddenly Slow: Poems

AS EDITOR

Deaf Lit Extravaganza

Deaf American Poetry

WHERE I STAND

On the Signing Community and My DeafBlind Experience

JOHN LEE CLARK

Handtype Press
Minneapolis, MN

ACKNOWLEDGMENTS

The author is grateful to the following publications, in which some of the essays in this book first appeared:

The Chronicle of Higher Education: "Unreasonable Effort."
Clerc Scar: "ASL Poetry as Novelty," "Great Expectations," "Paul Hostovsky," and "Why Hearing Parents Don't Sign."
Deaf Lit Extravaganza: "My Alma Mater."
Laurent: "ASL and 'The Star-Spangled Banner.'"
The Minneapolis Star Tribune: "All That I Can't Leave Behind" and "Does Disability Really Need to Be Fixed?"
Poetry: "Melodies Unheard."
Saint Paul Almanac: "Skyways."
Wordgathering: "Biting the Air Ahead of the Bullet: The *Wordgathering* Interview."

The author is also grateful for the generous assistance of the following while researching for "ASL and 'The Star-Spangled Banner'": Jean Bergey of Gallaudet University; Adrean Clark, Creative Director of *Clerc Scar*; Lawrence Newman, author of *Sands of Time: NAD Presidents, 1880-2003*; and Patti Durr and Karen Christie, faculty members in the Department of Creative and Cultural Studies at the National Technical Institute of the Deaf.

COPYRIGHT

Cover design by Adrean Clark.
Author photograph by Raymond Luczak.

Handtype Press, LLC
PO Box 3941
Minneapolis, MN 55403-0941
handtype@gmail.com

Printed in the United States of America
ISBN: 978-1-941960-00-4
Library of Congress Control Number: 2014945797

A First Handtype Press Edition

for
Adrean
and
our three awesome roommates

ON THE SIGNING COMMUNITY

ON LITERATURE

ON MY DEAFBLIND EXPERIENCE

FOREWORD

The title *Where I Stand* may be misleading, as the word "stand" typically suggests a fixed state. Either one is standing in place or he is taking a stand, holding firm. As a DeafBlind person, standing for me is almost never about being still or in one place. Waiting for a bus, I would move about without realizing it. My way of standing by moving around, I suppose, gives me more information about where I am. I'm taking in the scene, being present in the world, and prodding things a bit, exploring.

And when two DeafBlind people talk to each other while standing, they always move around so that, after a while, they're standing where the other person was. Later on, they'd be back to their former positions, having circled around each other. This phenomenon is the result of each person shifting to the left to listen to the other person tactilely in a more comfortable way, hand following hand at a certain angle. I would always find myself emerging from an engrossing conversation standing in a different place.

Writing the essays collected in this book was like that. I'd start out with an idea, an opinion, but by the end my position on a topic would be a bit different. Because I return to certain topics again and again, my thoughts would change from essay to essay. I would still be in the same general place—for example, I have always been horrified by the cochlear implant while also convinced that we will always have a signing community—but my precise position would be in constant flux as I gain new observations and my thoughts evolve.

To provide readers with a sense of my thought-movements, I've put the essays within each section in the order they were written. Although the contents in many essays overlap across the three areas, the first section concerns the signing community and discusses things that apply to the whole, including the DeafBlind community: what "disability" means, American Sign Language (ASL), the cochlear implant issue, and audism. The second section is more specific and tackles various aspects of literature, especially Deaf and ASL poetry. The third section is the one closest to "home" and deals with my personal DeafBlind experience.

While I don't expect my essays to change readers' minds, I do hope that they are engaging and stimulating enough to tug readers forward. Their positions may shift, either closer to mine or else I'd have helped them to disagree but in a deeper, more satisfying way for themselves.

J.L.C.
April 2014

ON
THE SIGNING COMMUNITY

DOES DISABILITY REALLY NEED TO BE FIXED?

Every time there is an advance in surgical audiology or genetic engineering, a wave of alarm ripples through the signing community. Doctors are intent on eradicating deafness. They subscribe to the belief that there's something wrong with being deaf. So they make it their business to try and fix it, hoping to ultimately wipe it out from humankind.

But those who are culturally Deaf are worried about the future of their language and their way of life, both of which are beloved. I can identify with their fears, because I was born deaf to an all-Deaf family. American Sign Language is my native language. I graduated from the Minnesota State Academy for the Deaf, where I enjoyed a rich social education and adjusted to my growing blindness. I went to Gallaudet University, the world's premier institution of higher education with a mainly Deaf student body. It was where my parents met and where I fell in love with a Deaf woman who became my wife. Although our three sons are hearing, ASL is their native language and they are members of the signing community as much as we are. I love being DeafBlind and would not change it for the world.

Like many Deaf people, I don't consider deafness as an impairment. Yes, there is discrimination and there are social notions and attitudes that disable us. But I grew up in a culture where we understood that deafness itself is never the problem. If there was a problem, it always lay elsewhere: in lack of access, denial of civil rights, or narrow rules and definitions. I have found this perspective to be true. Not even my becoming blind has changed the way I embrace this so-called disability as natural.

And not merely natural. It may even be vital to the human race. *Homo sapiens* has always included a broad range of shapes, colors, and other variations. While societies have established different expectations for what the human ideal is, all efforts to enforce one kind of normalcy or another have led to disaster and failed. No matter how misfits, defectives, and the afflicted may have been demeaned, rejected, and massacred they have always been inextricably wrapped up in the mainstream. Shouldn't we be thankful for the diversity that evolves among us, instead of arbitrarily deciding that one thing is normal and another is not?

What would our literature be without the blind poets Homer and John Milton? What would music be without Beethoven? What would the lovely French language be without the Deaf poets who launched the modern French vernacular? What would we do without the inventions of Thomas Alva Edison? And the thermos of coffee you are holding while you read this wouldn't have been possible without a prototype created by a DeafBlind man, James Morrison Heady. It was Deaf students who inspired their teacher to invent the first typewriter—he wanted to find a way for them to write as fast as they fingerspelled! Disability has shaped our world, along with other forces, and continues to touch everything around us.

Considering all of the above, I have to wonder if humankind can afford to eliminate deafness or stop it from running its biological course. I think the answer is no. Why not? Because when there are no more Deaf people, should that day ever come to pass, there will also be no more human beings as we know them today. If the medical industry succeeds in eradicating disability and perfecting the human race, it would have done something even more fatal. Already, millions of people who have no disabilities are demanding to be reshaped and remade. They are not satisfied with being merely well; they want to be better than well. I think this is a dangerous desire with potentially devastating consequences.

So I'm not going to worry about whether or not my community will disappear. I am confident that we Deaf people will be around for as long as human beings are around. That is because the two are the same: Inherent in what it means to be human is a wealth of possibilities that includes my deafness and blindness. Narrowing down the possibilities would limit human resources—languages, skills, and creativity born in diversity—available to the world.

Isn't *that* cause for alarm?

WHY HEARING PARENTS DON'T SIGN

One of the strangest facts related to the signing community is that most hearing parents of Deaf children do not sign. It has been said that ninety-seven percent of hearing parents never learn ASL. Why aren't more of them willing to learn sign language?

I used to have complicated theories about this, but one day it dawned on me that the answer is so simple it's almost shocking. Most hearing parents don't sign because they don't want to communicate with their children.

Think about it for a second. If they wanted to communicate, why, it would only be natural that they would sign. The problem has nothing to do with sign language itself, certainly not access to learning it or the challenge of mastering it. Millions of people all over the world flock to sign language classes. Non-deaf signers outnumber Deaf signers. In the United States, ASL is second only to Spanish in its popularity as a "foreign" language.

You would think that parents have even more reason, no, the *best* reason, to learn sign language. Instead, it is one of the hardest, rarest things in the world for a parent to do. Why is that?

Most parents are conditioned, from their birth up, for the simple reason they were parented first before they became parents themselves, to engage in a power and control relationship with their children. This is taken so much for granted in our society that very few people are aware that children make up the most oppressed and abused population. True, children start out in life as small, making them vulnerable to—even magnets for—all sorts of mistreatment, but that doesn't make them any less human or less deserving of respect.

Unfortunately, the Victorian view of children—"Children should be seen and not heard"—still permeates modern mainstream parenting culture. The biggest sickness in a relationship involving power and control is the absence of true communication. There may be a great deal of talk passing between parents and children, but a careful study will reveal that very little of it is real communication.

Because of their misguided belief that they must control their children through the manipulations of power, parents do not want communication to occur. They would find it immediately threatening. This results in their often saying things like "Don't you dare talk back to me!" or "Because I said so!" If there is true communication, it immediately elevates children's status, forcing adults to recognize them not as objects or second-class beings but as individuals with totally valid needs and desires that are just as important as their own. Few parents are prepared for such an egalitarian relationship with their children.

The power dynamics involved explain why fathers, in traditional hierarchical households, are less likely than mothers to learn sign language, and why the few signs they do know are non-negotiable signs of authority: NO, STOP, BED NOW. It also explains why hearing siblings, who are more or less equal to their Deaf siblings, are the family members most likely to sign. It's no accident that most of the parents who do sign are "different" from the mainstream mold—open-minded, eccentric, radical. They may not always realize this, but often they are not only embracing sign language, bilingualism, or the cultural perspective of deafness, but an alternative style of parenting that lessens or removes the "versus" in their relationships, replacing it with, well, "with."

Interestingly, the oral deaf community has the same problem. Despite their children's skills in lipreading, most parents are unwilling to accommodate their needs in this area. They still say "Never mind" or "I'll tell you later." But there are a few oralist parents who take care to look at their children before speaking, pause between turns, gamely repeat themselves, and take pains to include their deaf children in the family. I wouldn't be surprised if the percentage of such sensitive oralist parents is comparable to the percentage of parents who do sign with their Deaf signing children. But this is not a manualist versus oralist issue. This isn't even a problem unique to deafness. It's a much deeper concern having to do with parenting, power and control, and what it means to truly communicate.

Another interesting phenomenon is that some non-signing parents do learn how to sign . . . later, often too late. There are many stories telling of how a parent got a new Deaf coworker at the office, or comes into contact with Deaf people at church. All of a sudden, the parent is eager to learn sign language. Why *now*, after five, ten, fifteen, twenty years of living with their own flesh and blood? Simple: the new relationships with these Deaf adults are not stuck in the quagmire of power and control. Other stories tell of hearing parents' hands magically coming to life when they find themselves to be new grandparents of their Deaf children's Deaf children. This happened in my family. My grandfather never signed much to his Deaf daughter until the day he learned his grandson was Deaf. Again, the key here is power: The traditional grandparent-grandchild relationship is thankfully much less wrapped up in control than the traditional parent-child relationship.

That the medical perspective of deafness is relentlessly presented to parents doesn't help. The idea that Deaf children are impaired, in need of treatment and rehabilitation, only discourages parents from regarding their children as individual human beings worthy of equal respect and true communication. So the battle against audism shouldn't stop with changing parents' attitudes toward deafness, but should address the very nature of the growing people we call children. Why? Because parents can, and do, learn sign language only to exercise power and control over their Deaf children in different but equally abusive ways. Within the signing community, even Deaf parents need to understand what true communication with their children requires. Otherwise, they wouldn't be much better than all those hearing parents who do not sign.

The question to ask hearing parents, then, is "Do you want to communicate with your children?" If their answer is yes, there are no excuses for not learning sign language. No excuses. If their answer is no, their crime goes beyond merely neglecting to sign. Their crime is perpetuating the oppression and abuse of children, passing on the power and control cycle to the next generation, and the next, and who knows when it will finally be broken?

GREAT EXPECTATIONS

From time to time, I would be startled when one of my friends or acquaintances decides to "leave" our community. They are always non-natives, often people who found their way into our world as adults after excruciating childhoods as the only deaf one in their families and schools. One woman who recently did this said that "the Deaf community is a snake pit of backstabbers!" Another friend who walked out on my local DeafBlind community fired off a blanket email message accusing everyone of rejecting him.

The reason why their departures seem so sudden to me is that, as far as I could tell, the Deaf community isn't a snake pit of backstabbers and that the DeafBlind community did accept that man. These incidents remind me once again how differently people can experience the same thing, in this case, our community. So differently, in fact, that you would think they were talking about different planets.

Some who performed the Exit Stage Left act have suggested that they were mistreated and disrespected because they've been mainstreamed or because they don't sign ASL fluently. They charge me and other natives of being "insensitive." They say we are "lucky" and that the reason nobody stabs our backs or rejects us is because we went to Deaf schools and because we sign like water. (Never mind that we are subjects of gossip as much as anyone else.) Based on this argument, the community is at fault, and they've been unjustly forced to "quit" our community. (Never mind that no one asked them to leave.)

Now, I'm not saying that people aren't sometimes mistreated in our community. As a DeafBlind member of our predominantly sighted signing community, I am no stranger to being discriminated against or being avoided like the plague. Sexism and racism exist in our community just as they do in society at large. This problem of certain members abandoning our community happens even when these types of bigotry don't apply. There have been black Deaf members leaving black Deaf folk, DeafBlind leaving DeafBlind, feminists leaving feminist friends. How could there be such discrepancies in how people feel about our community?

If there's one thing that can make people interpret the same thing in opposite ways, it's expectations. For example, I visited a sculpture garden with a friend. This place had a famous piece which we would encounter for the first time. We found that it was seventeen feet tall. I was impressed, but my friend was disappointed. Why? Because I thought it would be only five, maybe eight feet tall, while my friend expected it to be thirty, even forty feet tall. Such is the distorting power of expectations. Could it be that some members, especially those who come in later in life, carry great expectations for what our community should be?

One sure way to find "evidence" that says there's something inherently wrong with our community is to have certain expectations for what would be "right" that our community should fulfill. Our community should be nice to everyone and accept everyone. Our community should not allow gossip. Our community should be patient. Our community should never condone labels. Our community should understand, should know better, should behave, should act more mature, should be more professional, should be more welcoming. Should, should, should. And since all of those shoulds refer to good ideals, we who love our community are at a loss how to respond. It's not like we can say, "It's fine that we are immature, and backstabbing is great!" So we have no answer to the bitterness, hurt, and rage bubbling up in those members until they leave weeping.

A quick consideration of their typical backgrounds—mainstreaming, lonely childhoods, communication deprivation—makes me realize that this background is ripe breeding grounds for great expectations. Human beings are social animals. When some are unfortunately isolated, it is natural that they should long to have contact with others. They talk to themselves, they create imaginary friends, they retreat into fantasy worlds. Games, movies, and books are easier to understand than real life. Doing homework on time and getting straight A's are safer than venturing out into the hallways and back lots and risking awkward situations or ambushes.

And then they meet other Deaf people. It's a new world. There exists a community! A culture! Could this—? Could they—? Yes, it's a family, and yes, they can become part of it and at long last belong. And this is great. It really is.

But ours is also an ordinary community. The social climate is, well, normal. There is normal competition. There are natural bonds and divisions. Love, hatred, compassion, jealousy, admiration, intolerance—they're all part of life in our community, as they are in any other.

Through my conversations with non-natives, I have learned that many of them grew up in a social vacuum where they did not have access to all the finer points of human interactions. This seems to have the result that some grow up with a thin social skin. When they enter the signing world, the first community they have full access to, they enter unarmed and are vulnerable. So things like rumors can be confusing and hurtful. They can become paranoid, worrying about what others think of them. They are afraid that everyone will believe everything that's said about them, and that they will be rejected, left out and left behind again. The ground beneath their feet can seem so unsteady.

When I encounter this mixture of longing and fear, I want very much to assure them that it's all right, that they do belong, that they are accepted, and to please not worry. But I have learned that this assurance cannot be magically given or surgically implanted in them. Our warmth, hugs, and encouragement can help, but this assurance, this security, this identity must be born in their very beings. Ultimately, it is their responsibility.

Sometimes they want our community to be different, to fit their idea of the dream community. It is true that our community needs to change, and always keep on changing, with the flow of our human needs. But our community does have certain social structures and rules, and it sometimes cannot accommodate certain attitudes and behaviors. While notions of universal peace and acceptance are beautiful, the reality is that our community's success depends as much on our flaws and limitations as on our virtues. In the struggle between the base and the ideal is life. It is up to them to reconcile themselves with the foundations of our community or not.

I think that an awareness of expectations is important for our making peace with this phenomenon. We who love our community should not feel bad for failing to meet those great expectations. No community on Earth can meet them. When members leave us, they will encounter the same humanity everywhere else. We hope that their life journeys will lead them to us again, this time with a richer understanding of who we all are.

ASL AND "THE STAR-SPANGLED BANNER"

"The Star-Spangled Banner" holds a peculiar place in the signing community. As Deaf Americans, our relationship with it is as complex as our relationship is with our country, a nation where we have been and continue to be oppressed and persecuted. We learn at an early age that all the talk of freedom isn't always about us. Consider, for example, what a Deaf high schooler named Julie Ann Lewis wrote in a poem called "Hear Me America" (1996). It closes with these lines: "My voice is not free— / How can this be / In this free Republic?"

On a more practical level, "The Star-Spangled Banner" is in English, which is not native to Deaf culture. Further distancing it from us, it finds its expression most often as a piece of music, sung at important occasions and sporting events. Even when the anthem is accompanied by a signed version, we have mixed feelings. On one hand, it is good to have signing displayed in public, something we cannot take for granted because of oralist campaigns in the past against the public use of sign language. On the other hand, "The Star-Spangled Banner" is almost never signed well or in a way that makes sense in our language. This forces us to wonder if the signing is there for us or more for the pleasure of hearing people who don't know the difference.

The Super Bowl is a prime example of this problem. Ever since Lori Hilary signed the anthem at Super Bowl XXVI in 1992, signed renditions have been part of the highest-rated television program on earth. This makes these glimpses the biggest exposure our language receives each year. They are much better for ASL awareness than the static I Love You sign. But are Deaf people inspired by these performances? Hardly. Only snatches of the signer are shown. Worse, most of the performances at the Super Bowl—and elsewhere—follow the same broken formula.

This is strange, because Deaf people have been signing "The Star-Spangled Banner" for a long time, since before it became our national anthem on March 3, 1931. The Deaf elite, made up mainly of graduates of Gallaudet College, enjoyed "rendering in signs" various poems and songs, as it signified their level of education and facility with the English language. Those who did this well were praised. Take this admiring passage written in an obituary in the *Illinois Advance* on the death of National Association of the Deaf's third president, Dudley Webster George (1855-1930): "He was a master of the English language and of the sign language. Of the correct use and beauty of both he was in precept and example an ardent exponent. No one who ever saw him address a meeting or render in signs the 'Marseillaise' or the 'Star-Spangled Banner' or any other poem will ever forget it."

We cannot be certain, without watching a film of George's version, how he executed it. But we do know that "mastery" of reciting poems in those days meant transliteration or something similar to what we today call Pidgin Signed English. Signers would follow the word order of the original English text, delete unnecessary bits like "the" and "of," and try to sign the words as gracefully as possible. No matter how impressive the bearing of the signer or how beautiful the sweep of the hands, it made little sense as an ASL text. If you taught a Deaf child only ASL, without ever introducing English, and he saw "The Star-Spangled Banner" signed, it would have no meaning.

Signed renditions, then, were not ASL renditions at all. Instead, they were a way to present the English text in "signs," in order that signers "read" the song in the air. This did not mean Deaf people weren't moved by the signing of the song. There is still charm and a kind of beauty in the signed versions, and through ritual use, it can become so familiar that it cannot help but resonate. Still, "The Star-Spangled Banner" has been signed again and again for over a century without much improvement. Why has the signed version failed to evolve into a true ASL translation?

The obvious answer is that the signed version has long been expected to accompany the music. The national anthem is signed at every graduation and before every sporting event at every pro-ASL school for the Deaf—which means thousands of performances each year—but all of them involve a sound recording and, often, a hearing "coach" leading the Deaf signers to make sure they keep time. While a translation, by definition, must needs be linked to the original, the demand that the signed version follow the sound has severely limited the potential for a meaningful ASL version.

The earliest known film of signing of any kind was of, yes, "The Star-Spangled Banner" being signed. Made in 1902 by the American Mutoscope and Biograph Company and labeled "Deaf Mute Girl Reciting the Star-Spangled Banner," the film clip can be difficult to follow because of its speed and jerkiness. But one can watch Susie Koehn's rendering, made in a clearer 1943 film, and be immediately struck by how alike the two versions are. And that same basic version is still performed today. Some new versions may appear to be better, but at closer inspection they use the same transliteration approach.

Amazingly, the 1902 signer got one thing linguistically right that none of the others since has gotten right: For "the home of the brave," the "Deaf Mute Girl" signed "home brave men," while most signers close with "home brave." But proper ASL usage begs the question "Brave what?" Of course, it is an old gender bias to think of the brave as men. A true ASL translation must resolve this issue of what or whom the word "brave" refers to or it must shift the concept. "Home people themselves brave"? "Our home inspire bravery"?

That all of the signed versions have since abstracted the meaning of "the brave" and almost everything else tells us that few have been interested in making the signed version communicate the song to Deaf people. The signed versions appear to have been and continue to be more a function of displaying the "beauty" of sign language to hearing people. This would explain why the accuracy of the signed versions as ASL pieces has never been a major concern. Moreover, the national anthem is most often signed when there are hearing people in the audience. It is rare for the anthem to be performed at Deaf-only, Deaf-run events.

If Deaf performers have been used as puppets, signing something that is meaningless in their language, it is no wonder "The Star-Spangled Banner" is not a sacred text in Deaf culture. In fact, ASL literature is full of hilarious spoofs and political adaptations. Patrick Graybill, in his one-man show for the renowned *Live at SMI!* series, apes his former hearing teacher's horrendous signs reciting "The Star-Spangled Banner." Mary Beth Miller has an even funnier routine in her own *Live at SMI!* video. She performs different versions, from opera style ("OOOooohhhHHHhh ssSSaaAAyyYY cccaaaNNN YYYOOOuuUUuuUU SsSsEsEeee") to fingerspelling alone in the Rochester Method ("ohsaycanyousee") to, finally, a sincere rendering that is similar to the one in the above-mentioned films. And the great ASL poet and activist Ella Mae Lentz has adapted it to deliver a political message. In her poem, ASL itself is the banner, persisting in the face of discrimination and language barriers. It closes by saying "Hands are still signing in the land of the Deaf free and the home of the Deaf brave."

As powerful as Lentz's message is, her poem is still heavily influenced by the classic abstract signed version of "The Star-Spangled Banner." For example, she still opens it with the dawn before awkwardly jumping back in time to the previous night by signing "Last night..." Nevertheless, it is a successful adaptation because Deaf viewers would recognize what it borrows from, the same old version that always starts with seeing something and then the sun coming up.

That the signed versions have been chained, sign for word, to the English version has not passed all unnoticed. The Deaf Pride movement did enlighten some people to a degree that they became uncomfortable with the traditional signed version. A new approach began appearing in the late 1990s at the more progressive bilingual Deaf schools, in which the anthem is turned into a kind of short play. Involving choreography, it features various performers enacting different things in the anthem—rockets, the flag—and taking turns signing bits. In some versions, the performers would sign the last lines together. These creative pieces are a bold departure from the traditional approach. Yet the theatrical nature of this method abstracts the meaning of the anthem as much as the traditional version does. We still lack a true ASL translation.

Which brings us to the question of how "The Star-Spangled Banner" should be translated. First, we must abandon the idea of following the sound recordings. The ASL translation can be signed while the music is playing, and with practice both can end at about the same time, but we must no longer think in terms of the two moving together line by line. The most necessary difference between the two would be moving, in the ASL version, the dawn to near the end. This move would allow us to, at long last, make use of ASL's cinematic qualities by first setting up the situation. This will, more than anything else, open Deaf people's eyes to the actual content of the anthem. To have a better grasp of the cinematic possibilities, it is instructive to know the story of how "The Star-Spangled Banner" came to be written.

It was two years into the War of 1812 between our young republic and its former mother country, England. After a victory in Washington, D.C., the British were advancing on Baltimore. Before they could enter the city, they needed to destroy Fort McHenry. The largest and strongest ships from the British fleet were anchored in front of the fort, their heavy guns ready to blast away. One of the prisoners onboard the Admiral's flagship was a beloved doctor, William Beanes. His friends wanted to rescue him and secured an official letter from President Madison stating that the good doctor was not a solider but a private citizen. Now someone had to go to that ship and present the letter to the admiral and ask for Dr. Beanes's release.

Francis Scott Key and another friend volunteered for the mission, and they went across Chesapeake Bay on a government boat under a flag of truce. They rowed right up to the flagship and were allowed to go on board. The admiral agreed to release Dr. Beanes but said that, unfortunately, they were about to open fire on Fort McHenry. He did not want the Americans to run to the fort and warn the soldiers there, so he charged them to stay away from the shoreline until the fort was destroyed. They could return to their boat and stay on it, and he assured them that they wouldn't have long to wait because the British guns would flatten the fort in no time.

That's how Key ended up stuck on that boat, at a safe distance from the fleet. He was not happy about this circumstance, because he was a volunteer soldier and wanted to fight with his countrymen inside the fort. He was also concerned for his brother-in-law, who was the commanding officer at the fort, and he knew the force there was small.

As night fell, the British began their bombardment of the fort. Key and his companions could not see anything except for the "rockets' red glare" and whatever it illuminated. Every time there was an explosion, they could see the stars and stripes flying. As long as the flag was still waving, the fort was still standing. But at some point during the night, the guns stopped, and there was nothing but darkness. Did this mean the fort was down?

Then "the dawn's early light" came, but there was a heavy morning fog. They still could not see the fort at all. As the fog thinned and lifted, there it was! The massive star-spangled banner was still waving! Key cried to his companions, "Oh say can you see!" The attack on Fort McHenry had failed. As the ships left and the Americans' boat made its way toward the shore, Key was already writing down on an envelope the lines of a poem. This poem was printed under the title "Bombardment of Fort McHenry" and was such a hit that it was being sung in New Orleans within six days, which means it spread faster than the postage. It had three stanzas, and the first stanza became our national anthem, but not before it was already our nation's most popular patriotic songs.

There is much in this inspiring story that can help us create a powerful ASL version that would make linguistic sense and signed as a true ASL poem. To begin with, there's the chronology, starting with the situation, the Americans stuck on the boat, on the sidelines watching the ships on one side and the fort on the other. The bad signed version doesn't establish this situation at all; the signer looks ahead and just signs. This leads to some contradictions, such as the signer talking about looking over the ramparts and then talking about seeing the flag. How can one see the flag ahead while one is also looking over the ramparts, a position where the flag would be directly above, not ahead of the signer at some distance?

An ASL version would set the ships—or, at the least, one set of the guns involved in the conflict—to one side and the fort and the flag on the other side, and the signer would refer to each side by turns throughout, with the default "narrator" looking ahead being the Americans on the sidelines, watching, helpless, hoping, and with the coming of dawn's early light, joyous.

Their joy can become our joy when we have "The Star-Spangled Banner" unfurled, full and clear, in our own language. We deserve that, for we, too, are Americans.

COCHLEAR IMPLANT THOUGHT EXPERIMENT

Let's suppose three hundred deaf people, all wearing cochlear implants, are gathered and moved to an island. None of them knows ASL and all of them have excellent speech. There are no hearing people there. What will happen?

I suspect that they will start signing before long and develop a new sign language. And this wouldn't be because they've run out of batteries. For this experiment, I've arranged for them to have an unlimited supply. Perhaps they continue using their implants, but in strange yet effective ways, such as calling for attention, sounding alarms, and maybe even sometimes communicating in some sound-based code or another. But their speech and speech-listening skills erode.

They erode because there are no people there who have normal hearing and can listen critically to implanted deaf people in a more or less standardized fashion. No one is there to give them the constant feedback they need to keep their speech up. Among themselves, their speech culture splinters and goes haywire. To reach a common ground where they can consistently understand each other, they use simpler and simpler sound units. Spoken English crumbles into a rudimentary code.

Because a code is no way to communicate with others on a daily basis or to maintain complex relationships in the community, they develop a language that everyone can easily access. Vision being the most useful sense they share—which they were born with, not implanted with—it is natural that this language is a signed one.

That's the thought experiment I conducted in an attempt to explain why deaf people who use cochlear implants are still Deaf people. Another thing that it reveals is that the cochlear implant is not *for* Deaf people. If it were, they would be able to, or even want to, use the implants on their own and for their own reasons. But the cochlear implant is for, and promotes the interests of, hearing people. It was invented by a hearing man and the risky experiments and sometimes fatal operations were legalized by hearing people. The demand for it is driven by hearing parents. It financially benefits hearing teachers, hearing doctors, hearing speech therapists, and hearing businesses in the industry. It is only at the bottom of the industry that we find the token deaf person.

Thanks to the "for hearing people" dynamic, the cochlear implant is in constant erosion mode for its wearers. I mean, if the implant was really for deaf people, they would take off with it, like jumping on a stallion and running with the wind. Instead, all deaf people with implants are "cases" requiring much labor and money and attention and training. Hearing parents and others who have direct contact with implanted children have to encourage, push, cajole, remind, and manipulate. Often this is subtle or even "natural," such as in the way that a group of hearing playmates would unwittingly serve as a system of keeping deaf kids' speech up. But always there is slippage. Rarely, if ever, is speech and listening to speech a self-generating, self-sustaining source of power for deaf kids.

As those deaf kids grow older, they seek out things that are for themselves, as do all kids. Identity separate from their parents. Independence. Indulging in self-interest. As adults, they make or try to make their own lives. All of these forces from within, which are organic, contribute to the constant falling apart of the cochlear implant for its wearers. In time, most adults are able to reconcile the pressures from within with the pressures, real or imagined, from without to be cooperative and to conform. Sometimes the former gains more ground, sometimes the latter secures a permanent hold.

Often, though, the same thing that happens in the thought experiment plays out in real life. That's because deaf children often find themselves isolated from and rejected by their hearing peers, no matter how close they are to being "hearing." They are already on their own private islands. Maybe, if they're lucky, they are on islands with two or three other deaf kids in the same school. They may still speak English among themselves, because it's what they know. But the more deaf people there are in one room, the more speech as a communication tool collapses.

That's one reason public schools make sure deaf students are as isolated from one another as possible. Even if all of the deaf students are good boys and girls, cooperating with the oralist program, their being together in any number poses a threat. It's too easy for them to build their own little society. But don't we all, deaf or hearing, seek to build our own little societies? If a deaf kid fails to do that in a public school, he either resigns himself to not having one or he seeks it elsewhere—in a gang, online, imaginary friends, or younger siblings and children whom they can bully.

Those who keep looking for a healthy little society of their own do find what they're looking for. No matter how hard others try to stop them from becoming "like those people," they have always and continue to gravitate toward the Deaf community. That's why the thought experiment isn't really a thought experiment. Three hundred Deaf people are always gathering and moving to an island.

The only differences are that there's already a language, meaning they don't have to create a new one from scratch, and they are not on a physical island in the middle of a vast body of water. Rather, they have instant, fluid islands whenever they are together. This phenomenon isn't unique. Even in this age of multiculturalism, different cultures, communities, and populations remain remarkably clannish. For example, in every Major League Baseball clubhouse, white players hang out with white players, black with black, and Hispanic with Hispanic, each group speaking its own language and listening to its preferred music. That's just the way it is. Why should it be any different for Deaf people?

What multiculturalism is really about are members from different groups participating in institutions of society at large. It's not about being isolated from one's kind and staying in a pretty mixed bag all the time. Deaf signers have proven themselves capable of moving about in society, in all professions, at every level. It has not been shown that deaf people who rely on cochlear implants are more successful or more socially mobile. In fact, research indicates they have more problems. But to humor those who believe in oralism, let's say that oral deaf people are more successful in society. Does that mean they have better lives? Not necessarily. Unlike not just Deaf signers but also unlike any other cultural group, they lack a "place" of their own where everything is *for* them, where every social aspect and cultural feature empowers them, where deafness as an issue disappears, and where they are just people. Sure, oral deaf people do get together, but the fact they use speech puts them at an automatic disadvantage.

Speech has never been and will never be for Deaf people. George W. Veditz had it right when he said, in 1913, that "sign language is the noblest gift from God for deaf man." So I don't think I need to worry about the future of deaf people. Those kids with cochlear implants are smart kids. They're going to find what is good for themselves. They're going to figure things out. They have needs that no one else can meet. I do shudder to think of the rising tide of anger and psychological baggage; they've done so much for hearing people for so long. Some of that anger has been and will continue to be directed against fellow Deaf people. That's to be expected, as the oppressed first lash out against their brothers and sisters before they confront their oppressors. This is nothing new to the Deaf signing community. It has always been open to newcomers, even to those who once attacked it.

All of this is an old, old story. Some have said that the cochlear implant is different, something new. It isn't. Maybe the process of finding their own place is taking a longer, more complicated route. But what's for hearing people and imposed on Deaf people has always eroded and failed. What's for Deaf people always comes out from under the rubble and into the sun.

AN OPEN LETTER TO AMERICAN HERITAGE DICTIONARY

Dear Editors:

When I learned that you had added an entry for the word "audism" in your esteemed dictionary, I was thrilled. I had been wondering when the word would ever appear in dictionaries. It was coined in 1975 by Tom L. Humphries to name the prevalent attitude and assumption that hearing people are superior to deaf people. The word became a wellspring of dialogue about the discrimination against Deaf cultures and languages. Since the publication of Harlan Lane's extended discussion on institutional audism in a book called *The Mask of Benevolence: Disabling the Deaf Community* in 1992, there has been a steady stream of writing, artwork, and film on the subject.

And here, at long last, was validation from a powerful source of authority!

Then I read the definition. "Discrimination or prejudice against people based on the fact that their ability to hear is impaired or absent."

The first half—"Discrimination or prejudice against people"—is fine. But the second half has so many problems that it cancels and defeats the meaning. Never have so few words set off so many explosions in my head. Let me take you through it step by step:

"the fact": This hints at a justification for audism, as it brings up the notion of there being something objective, something which cannot be helped. Discrimination is distasteful, yes, but there is the *fact* that . . . what? That there's something wrong with those people.

"their ability": By this, you are establishing a framework within which your readers are to understand victims of audism, in terms of their ability or disability. This is exactly what deaf people, for centuries now, have been fighting against. As the Deaf activist and writer Alison L. Aubrecht puts it, "disability" implies that there are some people who are "able" in every way. Since no such persons exist, the notion of "normal" ability is an invention, and a dangerous one.

"to hear": This focuses the definition on the proverbial box around the ear—that is, the deaf ear. The broken one, the one at fault, the one that needs to be fixed. The medical establishment likes to separate deafness from deaf people, because it sounds good to say "We're trying to cure deafness" and it sounds bad to say "We're trying to eradicate Deaf people and their cultures."

"is impaired": The term "hearing-impaired" is a favorite of hearing journalists and bureaucrats who mistakenly believe they are being politically correct when they use it instead of "deaf." Deaf organizations the world over have denounced the usage. Even non-culturally deaf and hard of hearing people are opposed to it, making "impaired" an absolute no-no.

"or absent": The whole history of audist literature and philosophy about deaf people and deafness is contained in this single word, "absent." The most relentless and harmful statement is that the absence of hearing or speech equals the absence of intelligence. Hearing people and societies have often seen, and continue to see, deaf people as non-beings on whom they can project their fears and desires. Deafness is a state of nothingness, of silence. It is death. That "absent," with its long history of destruction, should be used here to describe deaf people is truly appalling.

So that's what you have given us: An audist definition of audism. Do you realize that it is like defining racism as "discrimination against people whose skin is defective or discolored"?

The signing community has used various definitions, and I strongly suggest that you draw up a new definition based on them. "Audism is the belief in the supremacy of hearing and speech." "Audism is an audiocentric orientation, a system of advantages and privileges that favors hearing." I like a close rephrase of a definition the National Association of the Deaf proposed to

Merriam-Webster (which hasn't added the word): "Prejudice, stereotype, or discrimination based on hearing, typically against deaf people."

None of these definitions are tied to deaf people's ears, referring only to hearing in general. All of these definitions include those who are not deaf but who are still victims of audism, such as a hearing child of a Deaf adult who is forced by a doctor to interpret because the clinic won't provide a professional interpreter or hearing parents of deaf children who have to fight against school district administrators to get appropriate access and services for their children.

Audism is serious. It is in your dictionary. I ask that you make it right—by defining it without practicing it.

Hoping that you will take action soon, I am

Sincerely yours,

John Lee Clark

Postscript:

My letter was posted on johnleeclark.com on Saturday, May 26, 2012. It found its way to a wedding in Michigan, where Steve Kleinedler, the executive editor of *American Heritage Dictionary*, was in attendance. He immediately contacted me to say he agreed that a change was in order. Twitter and Facebook were also abuzz about the bad definition.

Steve invited me to join Tom L. Humphries and H-Dirksen Bauman in consulting him and an assistant editor. Steve, Tom, and I spent most of Wednesday, May 30, negotiating, much like a business deal. We reached consensus that evening with a two-sense definition:

1. The belief that people with hearing are superior to people who are deaf or hard of hearing.

2. Discrimination or prejudice against people who are deaf or hard of hearing.

The original definition was in the fifth edition, second printing version of the dictionary, and the revised definition went live online and in all *American Heritage* apps soon after and later appeared in print in the fifth edition, third printing version.

MY ALMA MATER

When people go blind, they are rarely in a hurry to pick up a white cane. They choose to train their eyes on the ground as they walk. Even after they begin to bump into poles and other people, they don't want to use the white cane, which would broadcast their blindness to the world. Some have been hit by cars multiple times before they finally unfold the metal feeler. By then, when their eyes are at last free to roam about again, they don't see much of anything.

Because I was born deaf in Minnesota, I avoided this fate. Not blindness, for I became legally blind when I was twelve and my vision continued to change until I was twenty-five. But I spent an unusually short season watching the ground before me. You see, it was my good fortune to be a student at the Minnesota State Academy for the Deaf, which happens to have some of the loveliest grounds I have ever laid my eyes on. It was this beauty that, in good measure, encouraged me to use a cane and retire my eyes to a life of leisure. This is not unlike how many Deaf people enjoy music, reserving their residual hearing for pleasure instead of straining at speech. The rest of what I needed to embrace my DeafBlindness came from the culture of the school and from my family, both of which were, and still are, proud to be "different."

Like many schools for the Deaf founded in the nineteenth century, my alma mater is on elevated ground so the poor unfortunates would be nearer Heaven. The campus rests atop a tree-filled bluff overlooking the Straight River and a winding road that soon intersects with the still-intact Main Street in Faribault, the seat of Rice County, about an hour's drive south of the Twin Cities. Sharing the same bluff but effectively separate is the private boarding school, Shattuck-St. Mary's, famous for its hockey teams and for expelling Marlon Brando.

Whether it was intended from the beginning and all along I do not know, but the layout of the buildings is in perfect tune with Deaf culture. At the center is an open green, which has a baseball diamond and some maple and oak trees beyond the outfield. Olof Hanson Drive, a one-way road and the first state "highway" to be named after a Deaf man (who was a one-time president of the National Association of the Deaf and a renowned architect and minister), circles this green. All of the main buildings except one more or less face this green and thus each other, giving the campus the feeling of an enclosed, almost secret garden. And it is a garden, with spacious lawns in front of the buildings, smooth white sidewalks, well-tended shrubbery, and green lamp-posts topped by white globes that shine orange-yellow at night.

The buildings are all of native limestone, smooth-cut where the stones meet one another but crag-hewn on the outside. Three of the newest were built during the Seventies, squat, saved from looking naked and bald by their dark wood-shingled tops. The rest, except two, were built in the early part of the twentieth century. Two of the older establishments are neo-classical masterpieces and are state landmarks. The limestone is still yellow on the newer buildings and it ranges from pink to brown on the older buildings.

The first building on the right of the curve that begins the circle is Tate Hall. It is a long, massive mansion featuring marching rows of tall windows with green shutters and white trim. At the end of either wing is an elevated porch with white columns and stone stairs on either side, going front or back. The main entrance has wide stairs leading up to tall columns supporting a wide Doric gable. If there were two marble lions, they wouldn't have been out of place. At the middle of the long slate roof is a white cupola. Tate Hall houses the girls' dormitory, the administrative offices, and the infirmary, as well as the old superintendent's apartments, now the school museum. James N. Tate himself dropped dead there in 1923—I can show you the very spot.

Past the playground near the south porch of Tate Hall, past a picnic pavilion, looms Lauritsen Gymnasium. Because of the way the two main entrances jut out a bit like the corners of a castle, with GIRLS carved in stone above one and BOYS the other, and above each at the top a gable, the structure has a somewhat gothic appearance. The fact that the large upper windows, where the basketball court is, are frosted adds to this appearance. They are like the heavy lids, half-closed, of a gargoyle.

When it opened in 1930, it wasn't called the Lauritsen Gymnasium, for Dr. Wesley Lauritsen had graduated from the school only thirteen years earlier and just in the beginning his long career, which included serving as athletic director and editor of the school's highly regarded and nationally distributed paper *The Companion*. He retired in 1962 in time to complete a history of the school for its centennial festivities in 1963. Until his death in 1991, he attended almost every home game, standing at the same spot where he stood as athletic director. It was only after his death that the then-current athletic director was able to stand at that ideal place, surveying the entire court, the bleachers, and the balcony above one of the hoops. When I enrolled, I quickly learned of Lauritsen's most famous saying, also the title of his editorial column, "Good Work Is Never Lost."

The gymnasium in its early days was such a jewel, with a court that could be divided into two still-full courts that colleges rented it for home games and tournaments. The University of Minnesota five played there, leading to some confusion in the local papers because both the university and Deaf school teams were called the Gophers. The Deaf school helped the situation by changing the name to the Hilltoppers. Because it proved difficult to design an attractive pictorial logo—they once used a hill with a spinning top at its apex, and at another time, inexplicably, a mosquito—the students voted in 1971 to change it to the Trojans. In time, the gymnasium ceased to be a coveted venue, but it remains a popular gathering place for the Deaf community, especially when the opposing team is another Deaf school. One wonderful part of the Deaf school experience is traveling to other states to play their Deaf school teams.

Across the lane that branches off Olof Hanson Drive and into Shattuck campus, with a Civil War-era cannon out in front, is Rodman Hall. It is where the students eat three meals every day and on the weekends the school is open to host home games against out-of-state Deaf schools. It is a squarish building with trees close to its two main entrances, again one for girls and one for boys. Not that boys and girls have to enter at the one or the other like they were required to do in the old days, when all of the boys ate at one end of the dining hall and all the girls at the other, but the boys' entrance is closer to the boys' dormitory and Tate Hall is closer to the girls' door. The cafeteria is on the second floor, in a high-ceilinged room with huge windows. The first floor is a student community space, called the Friendship Room.

It is fitting that Rodman Hall and Lauritsen Gymnasium are next to each other, for the men they are named after entered the school together, although Roy Rodman never graduated. Instead, he was hired as a janitor. Over his long career, he accrued such respect and status that he was regarded as the personal owner of the entire campus. Dr. Frank R. Turk, an alumnus and the Deaf youth leadership guru, loves to tell Rodman stories, which always illustrate the value of character and hard work. Legend has it that Rodman polished every single light bulb on campus, including the rows of high lights in Noyes Hall Auditorium, no small task. He protected the hardwood floor in the gymnasium with his body, not allowing a single outdoor shoe to tread upon it, not even if it belonged to a referee. During chapel on Sundays, in the days when most students stayed on campus for months at a time and the school still had such Bible talks, Rodman watched the chairs like a hawk, swooping down on anyone who caused a chair to get out of line.

About that cannon out in front: It was used to celebrate touchdowns in the days before football players wore helmets. Deaf people enjoyed hearing or feeling the booms. Our closest modern equivalent is the big marching-band bass drum, which some Deaf football teams use for counting up to snaps and for cheers. My football coach, Mike Cashman, a history buff, once told me that the cannon was abandoned and wasn't found again for many years. It is now home to birds' nests, and from time to time students sit on it or lean against it or take team or group photographs with it. Down from the mouth of the cannon, about five feet underground, there lies buried a time capsule. During summer school 1990, before I enrolled in the fall, we were asked to make this time capsule and to return in the summer of 2000 to dig it up. That summer came and went without anyone doing such a thing, and I suspect I am the only one who remembers. I suppose I am waiting for it to be of a decent vintage before I go out there with a shovel.

Next to Rodman Hall is the boys' dormitory, Frechette Hall, one of the three Seventies buildings with the dark brown shingles all around the tops. It has three wings, each one a two-story building with narrow windows. Each is connected to the central area via a hallway that is all windows and a roof. At the very center of the common is a fireplace. Not just any fireplace, but one designed for big fires, with a large circular concrete bed and a huge iron chimney like an upside-down trumpet coming down from the pyramidal ceiling, its wide mouth not three feet above the bed. Students hang out there, in spite of other attractions in the common area: the row of booths, a large TV, a billiards table, vending machines, and other things. Perhaps it is the power of the circular that draws them here, or the fact that it is bright but with indirect light.

Out in the back are a playground, a tar-and-gravel basketball court, and a limestone cottage, the home of the school's Boy Scouts troop. This being the rear end of the campus, the backdrop is dominated by trees. This is the site of my earliest memories of the school, from the several summer-school sessions I attended before I transferred there as a full-time student for my sixth grade year. Both boys and girls slept in Frechette Hall, in separate wings of course, but we shared everything else—the T-shirts we painted in the kitchen, the barbecues we had outside, and the pillows and cushions we sprawled on to watch "Star Wars" flicker on the wall—the reels had come from the National Association of the Deaf, which captioned films before captioning became standard.

The next two buildings we students almost never entered. The power plant, a military-style block with Eisenhower written all over it, is where the school groundskeepers and maintenance men lurk. They all were hearing men in my time, and I think they all still are, many belonging to the same families, and I don't remember ever seeing any one of them sign. Their wives worked in the cafeteria and, because of their daily contact with students, more of them signed. The school during my time there had only one Deaf janitor, a lady who was born in Taiwan. Because I had Deaf parents, she knew them and always asked me to tell them hello for her. I remember grumbling about there not being more Deaf people working in the cafeteria or in maintenance. But that they loved the campus was and is evident, everything there testifying to their care. The women cooked first-rate meals and one of them was a legendary baker of cakes. For them, the school must have been like, as it was for us but in a different way, a second home.

Tucked behind the power plant is the campus's oldest standing building. Erected in 1896, it used to be the school's laundry facility, where girls also learned dressmaking. Long boarded up and now beyond restoration, it will be razed sometime in the near future. Beyond the slowly-crumbling edifice is the same backdrop of trees, but with a faded sidewalk going all the way to the railroad tracks at the foot of the bluff, where the river glides by. If you pay attention, you will find an even fainter walk splitting off into the woods, ending at a fire pit. No doubt many sweethearts had their rendezvous here.

Back up the trail and back to Olof Hanson Drive, there is a pair of rectangular buildings opposite Tate Hall across the green. Mott Hall and Pollard Hall are on what used to be the original Mott Hall, the school's first large-scale building. Begun in 1868 and completed in 1879, the imposing structure was razed after it was declared a fire hazard. Many alumni thought and still think that this towering edifice should never have been destroyed. However, it had so many architectural flourishes that it made me dizzy when I first saw a sketch. I suspect that it would not have agreed with modern sensibilities anyway. The "new" Mott Hall houses a printing shop, a carpentry shop, and a metalworks and welding shop, all very important in the old days, when most Deaf boys graduated fully trained for trade work, especially in printing. Pollard Hall houses the offices that offer various special services, such as the state information clearinghouse on Deaf children.

Atop a gentle knoll is the campus's second state landmark after Tate Hall, an impressive domed building with two wings bent back so that it might look like, from above, a stubby boomerang with a ball at its elbow. Noyes Hall is named after the school's second superintendent, who served from 1866 to 1896. The nascent poet in me was often in awe of his full name, Jonathan Lovejoy Noyes. The main entrance leads into the auditorium, where there is a stage. At either side of the stage, in a recess in the wall, is a white bust, one of Tate and the other of Noyes. The central ceiling is the dome, where there used to be a skylight. Facing the stage and looking up, one cannot miss two massive paintings. A WPA artist during the Great Depression created these images. On the left wall, the painting is of a sunny day with a rainbow, some chubby clouds, and yellow-green grass—California grass, not Minnesota grass. In the middle of this idyllic landscape is a huge human hand, rising out of the ground like a mountain. The hand is dry and cracked. On the opposite wall the painting depicts a stormy night with bolts of lightning, but here the hand is smooth and luminous. I suppose the artist was telling Deaf students that struggle is good.

There is a balcony, with fixed wooden theater seats, but the floor of the auditorium is bare except when chairs are set out. The school proms and dances usually take place there. There is a play put out by the students every spring. Commencement exercises. Visiting speakers. And weddings. By state law, the superintendent of the school is vested with the power to perform marriages. Alumni, teachers, and staff have gladly availed themselves of this service for over one hundred years. How nice it is to have a friend, not a stranger, officiate on your special day, and how nice it is, if you are deaf, to have your vows read to you in your own language instead of through an interpreter! Noyes himself—with his large Victorian belly straining against waistcoast, gold chains dangling, and whiskers on full display—loved to perform on such occasions. The new superintendent, Bradley Harper, the father of one of my classmates, had wanted to become the first American Pope. That didn't work out, but at least he'll be able to do weddings.

Behind the west wing of Noyes Hall is Quinn Hall, where the elementary classrooms are. It has another, smaller auditorium, one more suited to presentations and workshops because there are steps along the entire length of the stage. So it is a popular site for practical, as opposed to formal, presentations and meetings. The rest of the building is low and something of a maze. Outside, the same wood-shingled top of this Seventies building also roofs two open-air passages, one leading to the back of Noyes Hall, and the other to the last of the squat Seventies buildings, Smith Hall, where the high school is. It is named after my favorite alumnus, Dr. James L. Smith, who worked at the school for exactly fifty years, from 1885 to 1935, as a teacher and then principal, and a longtime editor of *The Companion*. Like Olof Hanson and another alumnus, the investment banker Jay Cooke Howard, Smith served as president of the National Association of the Deaf.

It being Minnesota, it is no surprise that there are underground tunnels. Tate Hall, Lauritsen Gymnasium, Rodman and Frechette Halls, the power plant, Mott, Pollard, and Noyes Halls are all connected. Because of asbestos, access to the tunnels is now restricted. But they once were used often enough for strips of wet green grass to fend off snow for weeks in the beginning of winter. I remember reading an issue of *The Companion* from the Twenties and the school's folksy science teacher, Victor Spence, reported observing a robin and her nest of pale blue eggs on one such green lane, not yet knowing, it seemed that it was winter. When I was a student, I entered a tunnel only once. It was football training camp before school started. A vicious wind descended, and we were told that a tornado was coming our way. We scurried into Tate Hall and down into its tunnel. We were soon joined by the freshly-showered volleyball players, and I remember thinking how we must have smelled, sweaty and mud-streaked as we were, in our long-unwashed practice jerseys. But the girls seemed not to mind, and we all picked up where we last left off in our never-ending conversation and laughter, our faces and hands glowing in the gloom.

That I was born in Minnesota and not another state is an important factor. Playing football and participating in academic competitions in the Great Plains Schools for the Deaf conference, and thanks to my parents' tradition of stopping by at Deaf schools on vacations, I have visited many schools for the Deaf and also some for the blind. No other campus compares in character and beauty to my alma mater. Call me biased, but I'm not alone in this opinion. In one old issue of *The Companion*, James L. Smith, reporting on the proceedings of a teachers' conference that took place on campus, wrote of entering an empty classroom and noticing a message chalked on the blackboard. It said, "I have never seen a grounds of a school for the deaf so beautiful as yours." In those days, the school surely had stiff competition in this department, as the deaf baby boom of the Sixties was still in the future. When that boom hit, many schools were forced to hastily erect new buildings. For some reason, my alma mater's enrollment numbers have kept between 150 and 250 students through most of its history, allowing the campus to retain its basic layout around the open green. It was beautiful then, but it must be even more outstanding now, in contrast to all of the schools marred by the boom and its aftermath—stuck with empty buildings.

One of the best things about going to a Deaf school is acquiring roots. The first thing Deaf people ask one another when meeting for the first time is "Where did you go to school?" Often there is only one degree of removal between any two Deaf persons, so intricately and deeply connected is the Deaf community. Before we even met, my wife, from North Carolina School for the Deaf, and I shared at least three points of connection: The fact my father graduated from her school, our having studied leadership under Frank R. Turk, and our having both served on superintendent selection committees that hired the same person, Dr. Katherine Jankowski, who first headed her school before moving to mine some years later.

And no graduate of a Deaf school is a stranger to history. We are in awe of Deaf luminaries after whom our buildings are named or who grace the walls of our school museums or Halls of Fame. Because we are there, too, walking the same paths they walked, sitting in the same classrooms they did, and even meeting them in the flesh, we grow comfortable with history, with the making of history. When I went to Gallaudet, University, the leading historically Deaf college in Washington, D.C., it was already a familiar place with familiar names: The Elstad Auditorium, named after our sixth superintendent and later president of Gallaudet; the Hanson Plaza, named after Olof's wife, Agatha, the first Deaf woman to graduate from Gallaudet and one-time teacher at our school; the Washburn Arts Building, named after a Minnesota alumnus, the impressively-named Cadwallader Lincoln Washburn, widely regarded as the best dry-point etch artist the world has ever seen; and all manner of other indications of Minnesotan presence. Some years ago, when I was invited to give a series of talks at the National Technical Institute for the Deaf in Rochester, N.Y., I stayed in Peterson Hall, named after an alumnus and longtime teacher at my school, Peter N. Peterson. I haven't been there, but when I do visit the Southwestern Collegiate Institute for the Deaf in Texas, I will smile because its founder, Douglas Burke, came from my school.

As historic my alma mater is, the years I spent there as a student, from fall 1990 until my graduation in 1997, were among the most exciting in its history. It was the peak of the Deaf Pride Movement. American Sign Language linguistics and Deaf Studies were taught for the first time. The students led a successful protest that brought in our first deaf superintendent. The 1992 football team won The Silent News national championship honors. The

Academic Bowl team won five straight championships. And the girls' basketball team! Led by Nanette Virnig, the Johnson sisters, and the unforgettable Ronda Jo Miller, it won five straight national championships. Those girls went on to lead Gallaudet's women's team on an unprecedented run that garnered national attention, including two books. When Miller was lighting up Lauritsen Gymnasium, scholarship offers poured in from Division I schools, but she was only interested in Gallaudet, a Division III school. Hearing scouts, coaches, and reporters couldn't understand how she could sweep aside all those offers, but we understood. We all would have done the same. Miller finished her collegiate career as the all-time scoring leader in Division III.

I was there and I am still there. In 1993, a group of Deaf teachers were fed up with hearing teachers and staff speaking in their presence without signing. They successfully passed a motion to declare the entire campus a "signing zone." Signs reminding everyone to sign would be put up everywhere. They held a contest, asking students to enter logo ideas. My drawing won. It shows a green slope with five figures on it, silhouetted against a yellow sun, and above this two blue cloud-like hands making the ASL word "signing." They ordered a pile of those signs, and my art teacher, Bonnie Gonzalez, asked me to add my John Hancock to every single one of them. But I wrote my name in print, "John Clark." She asked me why I didn't sign my name with a flourish. I said I wanted to make sure people could read my name.

So I have many fingerprints on the campus. On entering the campus, one sees a huge sign—my sign—with the words "Welcome" and "Please use sign language." On leaving the campus, the last things one sees are two of my signs, on either pillar of the entrance pillars, with the words "Thank You for Signing." The signs are also in every building (except, probably, the power plant). But this is not how I want to close this tour of my alma mater.

I have mentioned football but not where the football field is. It is behind Tate Hall and occupies part of a long level field that includes tennis courts and more flat green behind Lauritsen Gymnasium. Across the street that borders this field are old-fashioned houses and beyond them more houses and streets. I wonder if, during all those years, the residents of those houses, sitting on their front porches, have wondered about what it was like to be Deaf and to go to that school across the street. All they can see, except for when we practiced or had games and the Deaf community came out to root for us, is the back of Tate Hall and the back of Lauritsen Gymnasium. Did they have any idea what it was like to be inside the campus, to be like me or Maurice Potter, after whom the football field is named?

Whenever I saw the aged, stooped Maurice Potter, Class of 1928, star athlete and many years a professional baseball umpire, at our games, I made a point to say hello. He always had an interest in us students. Some years after I graduated, I ran into his son, Jim, who was my math teacher and who had retired at the same time my class graduated, giving us a moving commencement address. I asked after his father and learned that it was near the end. Maurice could no longer drive or attend the home games. But he would ask his son to drive him to the campus, just to take a slow turn around Olof Hanson Drive. And father and son would look out of the car windows and, as I have so often done in my mind, take it all in again.

ON LITERATURE

MELODIES UNHEARD

The Deaf poet is no oxymoron. But one would think so, given the popular understanding that poetry has sound and voice at its heart. Add to this the popular philosophy that says deafness reduces human experience. As a result of such ideas, Deaf poets are often objects of amazement or dismissal, their work rarely judged for its merit beyond the context of their deafness. Deaf poets in America always have had to contend with sound, not only as a major factor in why mainstream culture considers Deaf people a lesser variety of the human race, but also as it relates to their chosen art.

This marginalization was especially acute in the nineteenth century, when demands for metrical verse were in force. Such requirements so discouraged Deaf poet John Carlin that he considered giving up on poetry. "I was convinced," he wrote, "that I could never be what I so ardently desired—a correct writer of verses." Fortunately, the perceptive hearing poet William Cullen Bryant pressed Carlin to continue writing poetry, recommending that he rely on rhyming dictionaries. Carlin eventually published many poems, including "The Mute's Lament" in the first issue of *American Annals of the Deaf and Dumb* in 1847. However, the hearing editor could not resist adding a note to the poem, marveling

> How shall he who has not now and who never has had the sense of hearing, who is totally without what the musicians call an ear, succeed in preserving all the niceties of accent, measure, and rhythm? We should almost as soon expect a man born blind to become a landscape painter as one born deaf to produce poetry of even tolerable merit.

In addition to this kind of treatment, Deaf poet Laura C. Redden experienced the opposite. That the acclaimed "Howard Glyndon," Redden's *nom de plume*, was a woman was well known, but few people knew that she was Deaf. When critics did learn of the fact, however, many of them lowered their earlier opinion of Redden's poetry. Infuriated, Redden responded with her 1870 autobiographical allegory "Down Low," in which she portrays herself as a bird with a crippled wing trying to make a place for herself in the fabled Realm of Singing. After some attempts, the bird wins an audience of soldiers passing through the forest on their way home. But when the soldiers discover that the bird is crippled, they abandon her, saying, as did Redden's critics,

> What have we here? A crippled bird that tries to sing? Such a thing was never heard of before. It is impossible for her to sing correctly under such circumstances and we were certainly mistaken in thinking that there was anything in such songs. Our ears have deceived us.

Any reader will agree that a crippled wing has nothing to do with a bird's ability to sing. Yet many will pause before applying this same logic to deafness and poetry. Even some Deaf poets themselves were plagued by doubts about their ability to write poetry, or at least "good" poetry that would be respected in the mainstream. Such doubts were, and still are, linked with audism, that is, the belief—imposed by hearing society and internalized by many Deaf people—that people with "hearing loss" are inferior. One such troubled poet, Howard L. Terry, wrote in the foreword to his 1929 book *Sung in Silence*, "In offering these poems to the public I feel as if I were throwing a snowball into a red-hot furnace!" Terry anticipated that he would not find many appreciative readers because his poems savored of old, of old formalism. In defense, Terry explained what he thought was the problem of the Deaf poet.

> Deafness retards daily mental growth. The deaf man slowly falls behind his hearing brother. He moves with the slower shore current, while his fortunate brother is hurrying along with the stronger, middle current . . . Equally gifted, the hearing poet is doing better work at thirty-five than the deaf poet. Beyond that age the deaf writer does less work than the other; he has lost his grip, he is growing less sure of his way as times change, and he is less able to grasp and comprehend the new order of things.

In contrast, many Deaf poets valued their deafness. They had long known that there was something beyond sound from which they could create poetry. Indeed, almost every other book in English produced by a deaf poet, culturally Deaf or not, since the beginning of the twentieth century quotes John Keats: "Heard melodies are sweet, but those unheard / Are sweeter . . ." But Deaf poets differed in what they took this to mean. For some, especially those who were not born deaf and experienced tinnitus, unheard melodies were the inner music in their heads. Robert F. Panara prefaced his collection *On His Deafness and Other Melodies Unheard* with "On 'Tinnitus' (Instead of a Prologue)," in which he wrote,

> I learned to count the blessing of deafness in still another way. This came with the discovery of Poetry and the realization that, at last, I had found that elusive nymph whose magic seemed to transcend that of her sister muse of song. Under her spell, the inner noises experienced a fine "sea change / Into something rich and strange" . . . Often, I would leave off writing a poem because I was overly absorbed with the melody I had conceived . . . Sometimes . . . these improvised melodies were so haunting that I would spend the whole night sleepless and find a better balance between a certain point and counterpoint.

Other Deaf poets had an understanding of unheard melodies wholly separate from sound, real or simulated. Deaf poet Earl Sollenberger, who wrote a poem called "Keats" in which he expressed his surprise at the fact that Keats was not deaf, believed visual experiences were equal to auditory ones in value. He presented both elements in his poem "Birds Will Sing" (1937), not surprisingly with the Keats quote as preamble.

> To a thrush on a mulberry bough,
> Once on a time God said:
> "Sing, little fellow, sing
> A sweet tune for that girl there
> On the lawn.

She is watching, she is waiting,
She is listening, listening, listening."

The bird sang.

At the end God said:

"That was a good song. My choir
Back home was listening in,
And I think that We
Shall have better music from now on.
That girl there
Couldn't hear you,
But she is satisfied too."

When free verse came into vogue, many Deaf poets were relieved. Free verse and other open forms were more than literal to them, they were physical; they freed them from rhyming dictionaries, syllable counting, and artificial pronunciation. Some continued to write formal verse but as a matter of choice. Despite the changing poetic forms, the twentieth century did not bring full liberation for the Deaf poet. The perception that sound is the elixir of poetry persisted, and the little publicity Deaf poets received continued to be more about the idea of the Deaf poet than the poetry at hand.

That Deaf people can write is obvious, as is the power of the written word in poetry. So why should Deaf poets still be considered a novelty? It is because of the belief that Deaf poets are always missing something vital. The physical voice is popularly thought to hold a higher place in poetry than the written word. Many hearing poets subscribe to this belief. Two examples will serve to illustrate this. Here is the French poet, Jules Supervielle:

> The printed matter that one follows with one's eyes, the silent and unmediated communion between the mute text and the reader, facilitate an unequalled concentration, the more precious because it opens up into an exaltation without witnesses. But isn't poetry made above all for the vocal life? Isn't it waiting for the human voice to release

> it from the characters of the printing press, from their weight, their silence, their prison, from their seeming indifference?

And here is Edward Hirsch:

> Poetry is a voicing, a calling forth . . . The words are waiting to be vocalized. The greatest poets have always recognized the oral dimensions of their medium . . . Writing is not speech. It is graphic inscription, it is visual emblem, it is a chain of signs on the page. Nonetheless: "I made it out of a mouthful of air," W. B. Yeats boasted in an early poem. As, indeed, he did. As every poet does.

Not every poet. Deaf poets have increasingly protested against such sentiments. Ironically, they can point to the same hearing poets for thoughts about how poetry goes beyond sound—"Poetry is a soul-making activity" (Hirsch) and "It is a question of inclining the heart more than the ear" (Supervielle). The hearing poets' statements about the sacredness of the vocal life may be only lip service, but it affects how Deaf poets are understood, or misunderstood, as they continue to write poetry, often as a political weapon.

For more than three centuries, the Deaf world has built a cultural perspective to contravene the formidable medical perspective of deafness that brands it as a disability. Indeed, the sixteenth-century deaf French poets Pierre de Ronsard and Joachim Du Bellay, even though they did not belong to a signing community, opened the poetical record on deafness by the deaf when they dedicated poems to each other reflecting on their deafness, and they did so in remarkably positive terms for their times. In his 1548 "Hymn on Deafness," Du Bellay wrote, "I will say that to be deaf—for those who know / The difference between good and evil (they are few) / Is not an evil, only seems to be so."

Much of Deaf poetry, even by deaf poets who do not consider themselves culturally Deaf, celebrates deafness as part of the human condition—different, perhaps, but still normal and equal. Moreover, their work is a collective subversion of the sound—or, to them, unsound—theory of poetry. Breaking the most ground are the Deaf poets who do not write. After all, writing is not native to Deaf culture as is signing. They make poetry out of handfuls of air; their lexicon is cinematic, giving rise to a new poetics. One fascinating advantage of sign poetry is that it offers, as Jim Cohn declared, "an even more open field for direct treatment of the object than English-speaking poets ever dreamed."

Other poets work with both written and signed languages, with a full range of pidgin and experimental work on and off the page, opening boundaries between languages. The late Deaf poet Dorothy Miles wrote in the introduction to her 1976 collection *Gestures: Poetry in American Sign Language* (book and video) that, with certain poems, she had "tried to blend words with sign-language as closely as lyrics and tunes are blended in song." She continued, "In such poems, the signs I chose are a vital part of the total effect, and to understand my intention the poem should be seen as well as read."

While audism, both in society and in poetics, continues, it is provoking stronger and truer responses from Deaf poets. Contemporary Deaf poet Pamela Wright was inspired to write "A Letter to C.F." after her hearing professor, in his opening lecture for a Shakespeare course, proclaimed that he pitied Deaf people because they could not appreciate "the beauty of language" without hearing the dramatic voice. Wright's missive in answer conveys what many contemporary Deaf poets feel.

Art starts in the heart and is meant to touch hearts. It is folly to think, then, that not being able to hear prevents a person from being inspired by sounds. The organ of the ear is a small compartment of a whole, not the whole of a person. Millions of nerves race through a body; what's to say a few in the ear destroy a person's ability to understand music? Or poetry? Or simply to have their hearts touched? And if the message is acoustic, is it always missed? Absolutely not.

Deaf poets have come a long way, but this should not come as a surprise nor a "wondrous irony." Sound is but one of many vehicles through which poetry can travel from feeling and thought to expression and understanding. In other words, sound is mere medium, not source. What is often forgotten is that the human capacity for experience does not wait for sensations, but it reaches out and fills itself to overflowing. Deafness can, and does, enhance the possibilities of poetry because it compels the poet, as it did Beethoven in music, to traverse roads less traveled yet toward the same destination, the destiny of all art. The work of Deaf poets serves as a prism through which Deaf people can know themselves better and through which the rest of the world can see life in a new light.

THE CASE FOR WRITING ABOUT DISABILITY

I love disability literature. But I can't stand most disabled writers. The reason is simple: Most disabled writers don't write disability literature.

Instead of following that old but vital advice, "Write what you know," most disabled writers seem to think their best chance at success is to write "mainstream" material. This is a sadly misguided notion, one that pours talent down the drain, the very talent that could otherwise have quenched the thirst of not only disabled readers but also the rest of the reading public.

The first thing to understand is that trying to write mainstream fodder is a joke. There is no such thing as the mainstream. Yes, groups have been and continue to be oppressed by other groups with more wealth and power. But no matter how excluded they are from the privileges and rights of the elite, every and each minority is part of society. We disabled people have always shaped the world around us, and our fingerprints on every aspect of life cannot be removed. To remove our presence and influence on American culture is to remove American culture. It would be a totally different world without us, as it would be without any other minority community.

So the "mainstream" is a myth. However, it serves the interests of our oppressors to promote this myth, to make it clear to us that we don't belong and that we are not supposed to try and find a place in the imaginary landscape called the mainstream. Thanks to the continual brushstrokes of doctors, teachers, and parents, this canvas teeming with "normal" people and expectations for "normalcy" can seem so real. But it's a lie.

When disabled writers try to produce "regular" literature, it is doubly false, shallow, and implausible. In a word: crap. To make matters worse, such material goes out there to compete against hundreds of thousands of pieces of crap produced by bad writers who, too, have failed to heed the advice, "Write what you know." The pieces of crap are shockingly alike, one clone after another—the same garish flatness of characters, the same stilted non-voice, the same lack of any connection to reality.

I should know. I was for seven years the publisher of The Tactile Mind Press, which focused on the literature of the signing community. Almost invariably, Deaf content was better than "mainstream" content, even from the same writers. Let me tell you about one story I got from a talented Deaf writer. It was set onboard the Titanic. It was well-researched, which imbued the story with arresting historical detail. Better yet, the writing was smooth and luminous. The story of the couple who had to be separated at the end was touching.

I rejected the story. The problem was that the Titanic, especially with a pair of tragic lovers, has been done to death. Only two things could possibly redeem such a worn-down subject—if a genius injected it with life by the sheer force of literary brilliance, or if there was a twist in the classic storyline.

What if the Deaf woman had written what she knew? What if the couple were Deaf? They are jolted awake when the ship hits the iceberg. They peek out of the door and see people running around in a panic. They scribble questions and try to have someone explain to them what's going on, but nobody stops to write to them. The truth dawns on them. A sailor tries to separate them, pulling the Deaf woman toward a lifeboat. They understand what this is, and the Deaf man encourages her to go, but she resists—the Deaf world is a small one, and going out there into the hearing world in a new land may be worse than death without the man who is not only the love of her life but also her guide to the Deaf world, because the man comes from a large Deaf family and is proud to be Deaf, but the woman is from a hearing family and never had the chance to go to a Deaf school . . . Will she insist on staying onboard to die hand in hand with him, or will she swallow hard and venture into the unknown?

Now that's far more interesting, and the writer would not have to be such a good writer to make it work. It's something new, and sheds fresh light on both the Titanic and the Deaf experience. This is why even the most successful non-disabled writers continue to forage for material from our own, poorly protected, territory. Many, many writers, from Daniel Defoe right up to the present, have made merchandise of disabilities. They may write crap, but it's useful, interesting crap and it sells. We hold a great treasury of possibilities in our own life experiences. So it baffles me and disappoints me whenever a disabled writer neglects an opportunity to stand out and instead just writes another "mainstream" piece.

Any disabled writer who writes what she knows, carving out visceral parts of her life, her very being, and sews them together with her imagination, is, right there, ahead of a lot of other writers. This is a mathematical fact because most writers are bad writers and most writing is crap. There are only a few writers who can write anything and it'd be important enough to be read for decades or maybe centuries. John Milton. Jonathan Swift. They were disabled and did not write disability literature, but they got away with it because they are Milton and Swift. You can get away with it, but writing what one knows remains the best writing advice. Take the supremely gifted African-American writer Richard Wright for an example: The only book of his that is not read is the one about white people, his attempt at writing a "mainstream" novel. Everything else he wrote is still in print and widely read. As wonderful a writer he was, his writing alone was not enough for posterity—it had to be his writing combined with what he knew, with the fact he reported on the world as he experienced it.

That's why I always let my life as a DeafBlind man flow naturally into my poems. Sometimes it is direct and explicitly political. Sometimes it is oblique. But it's always there. That's my saving grace as a writer. I hope that more and more disabled writers will do the same, because the collective narrative on the human condition desperately needs our stories and voices.

Let us write disability literature and in so doing write literature, period.

PAUL HOSTOVSKY

To read Paul Hostovsky's poems, particularly in his books *Dear Truth* and *Bending the Notes*, is to stumble upon something rare and wonderful. Too many gifted poets get sucked up in academic theorizing, causing their work to become unreadable, and too many poets who do write clearly lack the magic glue that makes words stick. Hostovsky has the good glue all over his hands, and interesting things have a way of ending up in them, including Deaf people and ASL.

In his day job, Hostovsky is a staff ASL interpreter with the Massachusetts Commission for the Deaf and Hard of Hearing in Boston, where he works mainly with DeafBlind people. In an interview, he told *The Main Street Rag* that:

> How I got into [interpreting and the worlds of the deaf and the blind] is the proverbial long story—which I guess is why I keep writing about it—but I guess the short answer is, I fell in love. First I fell in love with Braille, then with sign language, and then with lots of deaf and blind people, some of whom I have married. But for a long time I didn't write about it, because I didn't know how. I had tried writing about it, but the results were always either too sentimental or too esoteric.

It will help us appreciate the challenge that Hostovsky faces when we remember that hearing poets have been patronizing deaf people and romanticizing silence since before the Elizabethan age. In fact, poets have indulged in sentimentality so often while being so narrow in what they say about deafness that the English language itself poses an almost physical barrier against anyone attempting to write honestly about deafness and sign language. It is as if the English language has a mind of its own, and no matter how sincere our intentions, it is English's corrupt, audist blood that spills onto the page, not our enlightened views. Few readers realize what a triumph it is when someone writes fresh content about deaf people.

One way to do this is to take something tradition has used and turn it on its head. For example, hearing poets have often referred to birds and their song to dramatize, say, the isolation of a girl who does not hear the birds. It was Deaf poets like Earl Sollenberger who began catching the birds with their hands to make them our allies. From the Deaf cultural perspective, birds now represent signing, their wings becoming hands flying in the air. Hostovsky's poem "Feeding Nancy" is a fine addition to this new tradition. Nancy is his favorite ASL teacher, but she is now bedridden with multiple sclerosis, no longer able to sign. He visits her to feed her

> and to mourn the death of her beautiful
> eloquent hands
> lying heavy and cruel now as poached
> game at the feet
>
> of the heartbroken girl
> who taught those birds how to talk
> and sing—
> this is crueler than Beethoven going deaf,
> the loss
> of the music of these birds.
> It wasn't
>
> enough that her teachers
> at the school for the deaf punished the birds
> for singing,
> whacked them with a ruler, locked them up
> and let them starve—
> little cages of bone inside a cage—
> till her friends sprung them
>
> and they were happy,
> happy at last to be among their own,
> and they couldn't
> stop talking, and they couldn't stop singing,
> because this
> is the most beautiful singing the world has ever seen.

I love how Hostovsky brings Beethoven into this poem about an unknown ASL teacher, to say that what the teacher had to offer was, and is, more important than anything the world-famous composer could have ever hoped to offer. While such high praise for ASL borders on the sentimental, and would have been gauche in almost any other hearing poet's hands, the poem is grounded in the reality of the teacher having suffered oralist repression. So it is a fact, not a fancy, that her and her friends' liberation is so important that there are a few things in the world that is as important, as beautiful.

So this is a great poem in the Deaf bird tradition. Now what? What else could we write that would work? It is to Hostovsky's credit, and a sign of his commitment to his calling as a poet, that he didn't, couldn't, get stuck in just one mode. His work is a study in shifting approaches; he has poems that are entertaining lessons ("Deaf Culture 101"), philosophical ("Poem in Sign Language"), personal ("Deaf Ex"), and realist portraits that are also parables ("Dracula's Rat"). And Hostovsky has hit upon an ingenious method. As he told *The Main Street Rag*, this device is to take "the persona of the ignorant or uninitiated speaker." This has yielded some neat results. In "Away Game at the School for the Deaf," the narrator is a hearing high school basketball player witnessing the Deaf world for the first time:

> Maybe we were thinking *ears*
> instead of *hands*.
> Stepping off the bus, we glimpsed
> a flicker, then a flitting
> from a sleeve. We felt
> annoyed, then afraid,
> like spotting an ant on the tablecloth, then
> another and another till it hit us:
> what we had on our hands was a nest,
> a population . . .

Indeed, this approach works much better than a lecture. Maybe most basketball players wouldn't be so attentive and think much of going to a Deaf school for a game, but if a player did, this is what he would have thought. Maybe Leonard M. Elstad had the exact same reaction. He was on the Carleton College basketball team nearly a century ago when it played against the Minnesota School for the Deaf. The experience was profound enough for him to go on to study in the Normal program at Gallaudet before becoming superintendent of MSD and then president of Gallaudet.

Less plausible but still effective is "Deaf," in which a farmer is telling us about this Deaf boy who is good with animals. One day, the non-signing farmer and others circle around the boy, who is telling them about what he'd just seen happen on the road.

> He was the only witness when the
> neighbor's dog
> got run over, and he told us the whole story
> with his whole body, how the pickup
> swerved to avoid her, grazing
> her shoulder, the angle of impact
> throwing her into the woods.
> We all stood around, ignorant
> of what happened exactly, hoping
> and fearing as his story unfolded
> and he embodied first the dog running, then
> the truck braking, then
> the dog then the truck then the dog
> so we had the feeling we were seeing it all
> just as it happened, and just as it was happening,
> but in slow motion and with a zoom lens
> and from six different camera angles.

Even though signers are familiar with the cinematic qualities of visual vernacular, it is a bit of a stretch to think that someone ignorant of ASL would recognize this, much less describe this feature. But this doesn't matter, because it's still a poem that does its job well within poetic license, and non-signing readers will learn a great deal without thinking it is something they're not supposed to know until they've taken a workshop under Bernard Bragg.

"Deaf Love Poem" is another interesting example, but one with a different angle. Whereas the basketball player and the farmer talk about Deaf people, the speaker in this poem is addressing a Deaf person—in private perhaps, but the principle is the same—on whom he has a crush after watching her watching the interpreter in class. He notices that there's a lag in time between what's spoken and then interpreted in ASL, so that there is a "space" between the class's laughter and the Deaf woman laughing. He says:

> I want to slip inside that space and sit
> across from you, legs crossed, hands
> folded in my lap. If I made myself very
> small, inconspicuous, insignificant as
> another pair of antennae on the wall,
> just watching you, quietly, watching the
> interpreter, could I, could we, fit?

What I admire most in this poem is the delicacy with which Hostovsky presents the speaker's desire. Certainly a great many hearing people have experienced a wish to connect with a Deaf person, but equally true is how uncertain, how tentative they can be when they act upon this desire, if they do at all. That the speaker is in love makes this even more precarious. I suspect that Hostovsky was in a similar position before, perhaps when he first encountered ASL. But since that time, he has grown bold and assertive enough to make a valuable contribution to signing community literature.

There is one more aspect of Hostovsky's work I'd like to discuss. An example of this is "Little League," which was broadcast on NPR's *The Writer's Almanac*. The great Garrison Keillor read this poem aloud to thousands of listeners:

> When the ump produces
> his little hand broom
> and stops all play to stoop
> and dust off home plate,
> my daughter sitting beside me
> looks up and gives me a smile that says
> this is by far her favorite part of baseball.
>
> And then when he skillfully
> spits without getting any
> on the catcher or the batter or himself,

she looks up again and smiles
even bigger.

But when someone hits a long foul ball
and everyone's eyes are on it
as it sails out of play . . .
the ump has dipped his hand
into his bottomless black pocket
and conjured up a shiny new white one
like a brand new coin
from behind the catcher's ear,
which he then gives to the catcher
who seems to contain his surprise
though behind his mask his eyes are surely
as wide with wonder as hers.

As listeners smiled with the girl in the poem, it's a safe bet that no one knew that Hostovsky's daughter is Deaf.

And they didn't need to know. This is in stark contrast with other poems by hearing parents of deaf children, most notably Paul West in his collection *Words for a Deaf Daughter*. (Notice that the title refers to the daughter as an "a" and not "my.") Most have trouble seeing past their kids' "disability," or else they are unable to recognize them in such a way that their deafness is absorbed completely into their whole beings. The same goes for hearing lovers, colleagues, teachers—if a hearing poet writes a poem about a deaf person, it's almost guaranteed that deafness, or silence, or signing, or music will be central to the poem. Whether or not Hostovsky mentions a subject's deafness depends on the poem. His brilliant and humane discretion in this matter lends a wonderful honesty and freshness to his poems.

ASL POETRY AS NOVELTY

After the publication of my anthology *Deaf American Poetry*, I came into contact with a number of hearing critics and journalists seeking interviews or comments. Almost all of them were interested in ASL poetry, which pleased me. One leading poetry critic, a professor of literature at Harvard, upon learning of the anthology, immediately asked if it included ASL poetry and went on to say how amazed he was by ASL poetry. I was grateful he even knew that ASL poetry existed.

But then the attention lavished on ASL poetry began to bother me. For one thing, it was usually at the expense of the rest of Deaf poetry created in English. For another thing, their praise of ASL poetry is meaningless because they do not know ASL and, to date, there are only a handful of translations in English. How could they know that this or that ASL poem is amazing? Aside from the titles of ASL poems, they would have no idea as to the content. So why are they so interested in what they have no access to while dismissing the English poems by Deaf poets open to them?

The case of Paul Laurence Dunbar can, I think, help us answer this mystery. He was a hearing black poet born in 1872 who became our nation's first black professional man of letters, although his career was cut short when he died of tuberculosis in 1906. He is now best known for his poetry. He wrote in two general styles, traditional verse in standard English and poems in black dialect. In 1896, the country's most important literary critic, William Dean Howells, did a review in *Harper's Weekly* of Dunbar's second book of poems. Howells praised his dialect poems by writing, "[He] has been able to bring us nearer to the heart of primitive human nature in his race than any one else has yet done." Of Dunbar's work in standard English, Howells said there was nothing "especially notable . . . except for the Negro face of the author."

Howells's distasteful treatment notwithstanding, Dunbar was thrilled. The review drew much attention and helped sales. But he soon began to realize how this praise of his dialect work and dismissal of the rest of his efforts limited him. He lamented to a friend in a letter: "One critic says a thing and the rest hasten to say the same things, in many cases using the identical words. I see very clearly that Mr. Howells has done me irrevocable harm in the dictum he laid down regarding my dialect verse." Indeed, Howells had set the framework within which Dunbar's and other black poets' work would be debated for many years among literary scholars.

But even if Howells had never written that review, I think black poets' work would still have been discussed in a narrow and superficial way. The prevailing racism would have made sure of that. The dialect poems, being a cute novelty, would have seemed to reinforce white people's views of black people. Even a blue-blooded Klansman would have smiled benevolently while reading a poem like "Song of Summer," whose first four lines are:

Dis is gospel weathah sho'—
Hills is sawt o' hazy.
Medahs level ez a flo'
Callin' to de lazy . . .

It was not that Dunbar's dialect poems did not challenge racist sentiments. The charm of the dialect itself made it easier for white readers to deflect Dunbar's challenge, without knowing that they were denying his message. When the message is expressed in standard English, however, it may have been harder to deny. In fact, some of Dunbar's poems would have seemed downright unpatriotic and treasonous. Take the first stanza of his early poem "Ode to Ethiopia":

O Mother Race! to thee I bring
This pledge of faith unwavering,
This tribute to thy glory.
I know the pangs which thou didst feel,
When Slavery crushed thee with its heels,
With thy dear blood all gory.

The black community loved such poems. When Dunbar met Frederick Douglass, who was then U.S. Ambassador to Haiti, the great man asked the young poet to read "Ode to Ethiopia" first of all. But I can just imagine well-meaning white law clerks squirming in some discomfort while listening to the poet read these lines.

Is something similar happening today, with ASL poetry being automatically praised while the standard English poems are largely ignored? Could it be that some hearing critics, in their ignorance or bigotry, are unwilling to listen to the cultural, anti-medical perspective from which many Deaf poets write? Perhaps. I suppose an audist would not like reading a poem like James William Sowell's "The Oralist" (1913):

All you care to do on earth is to make a show,
    Claim the power of miracle to see the people stare;
For you have an audience everywhere you go,
    Oralist, whose traffic is a little child's despair.

Oralist, O oralist, show your silken hose,
Little souls are sacrificed that you may wear such clothes;
Little souls and beautiful, pure from God's own hand;
Halting feet that lamely walk; wistful eyes that plead,
Hearts but could you only read them, could you understand,
You would throw away your creed and give to them their need.

Oralist, O oralist, work to get your laws
Force the baby lips to lisp, laugh at all their flaws.
Minds they have as sound as yours but for hours you waste;
    Spirits as impervious yearning for the light;
See! Their baby hands they lift, pleading that in haste
    You may see the wrong you do and will cease to smite.

Oralist, O oralist, turn your head aside,
Know you not the pitying Christ for sins like yours has died?

As neat as the comparison between black poetry and Deaf poetry may be, there is one major difference that makes Deaf poetry's predicament worse. Unlike white critics, hearing critics don't even have access to ASL poetry, at least not yet. They do not know what the ASL poets are saying. They do not know whether an ASL poet is being ironic, earnest, brilliant, or pedestrian. They cannot begin to consider the art being displayed before their waxen eyes. This means the very idea of ASL poetry, nothing more, is enough. The novelty alone satisfies their notions of Deaf people as different, strange, freakish, a special class whose language is "beautiful."

But the blame cannot rest on hearing people's shoulders alone. Those who should know better are not helping matters any. The academic literature on ASL poetry is quite large. But even for knowledgeable scholars, ASL poetry remains a linguistic novelty. For them, the very possibility of poetry being created in ASL is enough. In the meantime, there has been very little study made of Deaf poetry—not only the poems that are in English but also the actual cultural content of ASL poems.

And many ASL poets themselves, in their own way, handle their work as if it is very special. It is natural for a poet to hold dear her own creations, but that's not what I mean. One way in which they keep ASL poetry sealed in its novelty status is by refusing to allow their work to be translated into English. Almost all of the people I know who have created ASL poems say their poems cannot be translated. What they may not realize is that refusing translation means refusing literature itself. As Edith Grossman explains in her book *Why Translation Matters*:

> they are absolutely inseparable, and, in the long run, what happens to one happens to the other . . . And their long-term relationship, often problematic but always illuminating, will surely continue for as long as they both shall live."

Yes, translating ASL poetry would mean mangling it. But it will be a confirmation of the original, and translation would help us understand ASL poetry in ways we cannot understand it when it stands alone. Perhaps because many ASL poets encountered doubts in others as to whether ASL is a language, not to mention skepticism as to whether their work is really poetry, they feel defensive, protecting it by exalting it to the skies, as something pure and untouchable. I sympathize, but it is well past time we understand that ASL is a mere language, one of many lowly, earth-bound languages in the world, made of magic, certainly.

Do hearing critics and audiences want translations of ASL poetry? Not really. Remember, the very idea of ASL poetry is enough, and they are happy. They do not want more because they have no idea what they may be or may not be missing. But if there are more ASL poems available with rich full translations, their very availability will attract, intrigue, and compel deeper responses.

We in the signing community are also to blame for ASL poetry's being trapped in limbo. There are two things we are doing wrong. First, we praise ASL poetry too readily. I shall never forget one lecture on Deaf poetry I was presenting at St. Catherine University. I performed, on purpose, a lousy ABC poem about baseball. It was just the various motions of a baseball game. I may have executed it with some grace, and it may have been a good exercise, but it had no message or any other redeeming literary qualities. Yet my predominantly Deaf audience cheered. Most of ASL poetry being produced are mere exercises in this way—dazzling eye candy, but no meat.

We need to become more discriminating, praise what is good, smile politely at what is mediocre, and blast what is bad. We need to watch more ASL poetry and develop refined tastes, thus creating higher expectations and challenging poets to compete. Put simply, we need to *want* better ASL poetry. Then better ASL poetry will be created.

The second way in which we do ASL poetry harm is by thinking that we cannot create it ourselves. After the pioneering generation of ASL poets—Ella Mae Lentz, Clayton Valli, Peter Cook, Patrick Graybill, and Debbie Rennie—there was... nobody. No one has come forward to create a body of work remotely approaching the quality or breadth of any of those poets. We seem to be in such awe of ASL poetry that we have decided it is beyond our abilities. I confess I thought I could not possibly create an ASL poem, but I have since learned that ASL poetry is just one way to express myself in ASL, just as writing poetry is one way to play with the English language. One doesn't have to be a Shakespeare to enjoy writing poetry; one doesn't have to be a Valli to sign some things differently for the sheer joy of it.

I think we can learn a lesson from the sixteenth century. Most of the poetry was written in Latin by educated clergymen and aristocrats. Then two French poets, Pierre de Ronsard and Joachim Du Bellay, both deaf, along with three other poets, helped to break down the ivory wall around poetry. What they did was use common French vernacular to write poems that anyone in France could read or listen to. This led to poetry emerging from people in all walks of life. Today kindergarteners dabble in poetry at school everywhere. Of course, very little poetry wins wide recognition, but poetry serves many functions other than attaining fame.

Now, the elegance and dynamite with which the pioneering ASL poets performed their work still impresses me and overwhelms me. But I believe ordinary ASL diction can make for ASL poetry that is just as great. Much of the best contemporary poetry in English is written in language that is stubbornly plain, free of flourishes. Perhaps my poem "Rebuilding" is a good example, not of what is best but of plain language being used in a poem:

> My grandfather spanked her. Half of the time
> she didn't know why. He didn't have the signs
> to tell her. After she got married and gave birth
> to three deaf children, he wanted to say something
> to us. His hands creaked to life. Buildings
> were all he could tell us about. The sod hut
> he was born in. The red barn on the farm.
> The basement he put his family in while building
> a house above their heads. The Ramsey Hospital
> where he was foreman and where I and my sons were born.
> The Ramsey County Jail we always pointed out
> on our way to visit Grandma and Grandpa.
> The bird houses in his green garden.
> It didn't matter what kind of building
> it was, as long as it was with his hands.

This poem is so plain it is almost not a poem. But, somehow, a subtle pattern, a bit of compression, one or two small choices make it a poem. What I am trying to say is that poetry is not far from what we sign every day. A few small steps can turn a casual account into a powerful poem. It is not hard, and I would love it for there to be more ASL poems that use colloquial ASL. We can still have fancy signing, but there should be more than that.

How wonderful it is that our language yields itself so easily to poetry. Poetry is already in our hands, if only we would believe that it is there and that we can and should bring it out into the open. Yes, much of it would be unworthy of wide attention. Yes, audism will dictate the dialogue about our community's poetry for a while yet. Yes, it will take a long time for translations to become widely available. Yes, the next generation will be slow in coming. But, at this very moment, what we can do is get our hands a little dirty playing in the mud of poetry, making it less of a novelty and more natural to us.

BITING THE AIR AHEAD OF THE BULLET: THE WORDGATHERING INTERVIEW

Michael Northen, the editor of Wordgathering, *the leading magazine of disability culture poetry, interviewed John Lee Clark soon after his anthology* Deaf American Poetry *was published in 2009. It was conducted via e-mail over several days.*

John Lee Clark: I have never been afraid of biting the bullet, much less biting the air ahead of the bullet. So allow me to jump in before you even fire your first question. Let's start with a glimpse of my office. It's in one corner of the bedroom my wife and I share. My desk is a wooden board with four metal cylinders supporting it. On the center sits my Dell laptop. It, in turn, sits atop my Braille display, a Tieman Voyager 44. To the left is a scanner. I use it to turn books into text files I can then read on the laptop or transfer to my Braille Wave, which I use for reading when I'm away from my office. To the right is a LaserJet printer covered in dust. The last time I used it was three, four months ago. On the floor is a brown paper bag. Inside are library books, which I return after scanning them.

Aside from my chair, that's it. Pretty Spartan, isn't it? I imagine my chair makes it seem more so, because it has no back. I've been meaning to buy a new one with a back, but other things keep on snatching away the money. Although we are not starving, this does help me appreciate what a DeafBlind poet, Howard L. Terry, once wrote: "A poet is a thing that starves."

***Wordgathering*:** Was it the Spartan nature of living as a poet that led you into editing *Deaf American Poetry*?

JLC: It is true that most all poets have to have a job other than being a poet. Mine is as an independent contractor who offers copy and content editing services. My clients include writers, scholars, and publishers. That's how I make my sporadic living.

As for assembling *Deaf American Poetry*, that was a personal project. I actually set out looking for materials by DeafBlind writers. But I kept coming across Deaf poets in my research. I soon realized that there needed to be another anthology, the materials were so rich. Although there were already whole shelves full of Deaf Studies titles, an anthology of Deaf poetry was absent. So I added this project to my main one. I finished it first, which makes sense when you consider that I focused on American Deaf poets only, whereas my DeafBlind project is international in scope, requiring translations from many languages. It's a massive work. I'm happy to report that it's almost finished. It includes prose as well as poetry: memoirs, essays, polemics, letters, and selections from diaries. It begins with poems from a 1788 collection. I'm very excited, as you can imagine.

WG: Is there anything that particularly surprises you about the material you are finding in your work on DeafBlind authors? Who are some of the most important DeafBlind poets?

JLC: I am more pleased than surprised. This is because I was given advance notice on how much material there is. In 1972, Terry Batson and Eugene Bergman put together a book called *The Deaf Experience: An Anthology of Literature by and about the Deaf*. They enlisted the help of Gallaudet's librarian in compiling a comprehensive bibliography. In the preface to this list it was noted that DeafBlind authors have written so many books that they couldn't be listed. They had to exclude those books. While this did make it harder for me to launch my research—that book, along with Jack Gannon's 1980 book *Deaf Heritage*, is the place to start for almost any research project related to the literature of the Deaf community—I have come to understand why it was necessary to exclude DeafBlind authors. In spite of the DeafBlind population being a fraction of the Deaf population, DeafBlind writers have written just as many books as Deaf authors have, if not more.

One of the big questions my research is seeking to answer is: Why have so many DeafBlind people turned to writing? One answer is that writing is a way to stave off isolation. Prisoners, for example, do regularly find solace and a kind of freedom in writing. Though we didn't choose to be isolated, and it's wrong for society to make itself inaccessible to us, it is possible to empower oneself in this situation anyway. As the hearing-sighted

Canadian poet A. F. Mortiz puts it, "When we turn isolation into solitude by being creative and seeking ways to make this the basis of social life, we are poets."

The distinction between isolation and solitude is an important one. Isolation is imposed, whereas solitude is a choice. Making the best of isolation is a logical human response to it. For the DeafBlind community, writing offered a particularly satisfying way to not only turn isolation into solitude but also create a social, political life by having their writings communicate with the world. And to each other. Before DeafBlind people began to get together locally in the Twenties and for national conventions in the late Sixties, there already existed a community, a virtual one, through many publications and correspondence clubs. Almost every aspect of social life was conducted through writing, including meeting others, becoming friends, dating, feuding, rooting for sports teams, celebrations of birthdays and milestones, weddings, funerals, running for office or editorships, and church services. If you saw a film montage showing all of those people sitting at their desks tapping away on their Braillers, you would have no idea that this one is a sportscaster responsible for keeping the DeafBlind community posted on box scores, that another is a minister who writes homilies, that a man in England and a woman in Utah are having a courtship and excitedly planning their first meeting in person after "dating" for two years. And you know what? This virtual community still exists, more than one hundred years old, only it has moved to email discussion lists. There is a list for every imaginable topic in the DeafBlind community. Writing remains the community's best way to empower itself and maintain a social life.

It's no wonder, then, that I have plenty of material to work with!

The best writing will blow your mind away. I promise you that. Interestingly, the first two Americans—Laura Bridgman and James Morrison Heady—are only the fifth and sixth in the book, preceded by three Europeans and one writer from Japan. Heady made quite a name for himself and is still a local historical figure of note in Louisville, Kentucky. But the four most successful DeafBlind poets, in terms of books published and other publication credits and awards, would be Evelyn M. Watson, a close contemporary of Helen Keller's; R. C. Scriven, who wrote many verse plays for BBC Radio 4 in the Sixties and Seventies; Robert J. Smithdas, the first DeafBlind person to earn a master's degree; and the eccentric, self-proclaimed "erotic mystic" poet from Cornwall, Jack Clemo. Right now, that's the Mount Rushmore of DeafBlind poetry.

From the very beginning, DeafBlind writers have coped with their condition in empowering ways. Getting to know them helped me respect even more the human spirit, its natural drive to secure as much power as possible, to achieve the highest possible standard of living. I've read some academic and other critical work on disability literature, and many seem to think that empowerment happened suddenly, with this or that movement. But what my research has shown me is that it's a much more gradual, steady process. I suppose disability literature is like sex. Every new generation thinks it invented sex. But if that was true, then how on earth did that new generation come to be? No matter how ignorant we may be of our predecessors' literary work, we have much to owe them for what we are writing now. It's good if we have direct access to older works, but this directness isn't a requisite for their influence on us today. The influence is still there. Nothing we do is entirely new.

WG: It sounds as though, despite it being a look at the work of DeafBlind poets across the globe, you are also going to take an historical approach, much as you did in *Deaf American Poetry*. I'm wondering if, in looking at non-American poets, you find that they have a different perspective or come with a different approach. I'm thinking, for example, of deaf Nigerian poet Osumon Sylvester who makes a great deal in his poetry of the way that the church in Nigeria held him up as an example of God's punishment and how he had to deal with the ethical stigma attached to being deaf. Do you find a different kind of difference in DeafBlind writers from other cultures?

JLC: DeafBlind writings from different cultures are different only to a limited, superficial degree. The example you cited—a disabled person being set aside or rejected because he is seen as a manifestation of evil—has its parallels in other cultures, including our own society in America. It just has a different shape, and the periods of time may vary from one culture to another for when there is more or less tolerance, more or less education, increased or reduced access and services. In spite of larger social forces, however, DeafBlind people are remarkably consistent in moving away from believing that there's something wrong with them toward believing that their limitations are imposed by their societies. Some writers would, of course, internalize the lie that there is something wrong with them, internalizing this so deeply that they believe in it their entire lives. But most come to the realization that there's really nothing wrong with them and they begin to assert themselves as human beings. This dawning has come to writers from all points in time since the first writer, from all countries, no matter what cultural trappings there may be. In Japan, for example, women put a premium on their ability to cook for the family. In America, driving a car is a huge symbol of independence. When someone becomes deaf or blind or both at the same time, it seems devastating because at first they don't know how they can still cook and drive a car. But if they have the normal human resourcefulness, in time they will realize that they still can cook, or travel, or do anything. How well they do it or not, and in what ways, would not be connected with their DeafBlindness but with what resources they have, what they need that society may or may not provide or allow. Always there is this same drive, going in the same direction. It's the same direction mankind has taken since Adam and Eve put on their first clothes.

Aesthetics: The poems themselves come in all styles. Some formal, some free. Some written, some signed. The interesting things are in the content of the poems. Themes that have emerged are explorations of the tactile-kinesthetic world we live in, orientation and mobility, communication, the various forms of oppression and manipulation we experience, childhood memories of sounds and sights if the poet became deaf and blind later in life, and, what strikes me as the most important one, relationships with others, especially significant others. In many countries, DeafBlind people do not find it easy to get into intimate relationships that result in marriage or partnership. While there may be no laws against them doing so, their families may be against the idea. If there are limited services, poor or no transportation, they are unfortunately dependent on their families, and so their families wield great power. But then again, in those same countries, families wield a great deal of power over everyone and all aspects of life. Still, finding companionship is one of the most vital, enduring human needs. The poems that deal with this, then, are usually the most passionate.

Back to the matter of the styles used in the poems, it's possible that DeafBlindness plays a role in how some of the poems are written. Unfortunately, I can't ask most of the poets in the book about this. I can only speak for myself. I wrote most of the poems in my chapbook, *Suddenly Slow*, using large print. I've been reading Braille since age seven, but it wasn't until I was twenty-six that I was able to get my first Braille display for my computer. I had long wanted it, but the state wouldn't provide me with one, saying I had enough sight to read large print. Translation: "The Braille display is expensive, so we want you to use large print for as long as you can possibly bear it." As a starving poet, I couldn't just go and buy one myself. So I was forced to use large print. Until I finally got my Braille display, I didn't know how much difference reading and writing methods made on the shape and style of my poems. In Braille, my poems have grown shorter and shorter. The lines are somewhat longer and I no longer use stanzas at all. Part of this may be due to the natural development of my work, but I am convinced the switch to Braille played a big role.

WG: How do you think that being Deaf and blind has affected your development as a poet? I'm thinking about Dan Simpson's essay "Line Breaks the Way I See Them" in which he describes how he was asked by the poet Molly Peacock why, as a blind poet, he was worried about visual line breaks in his poems. Does being blind affect the kind of poetry you write or the way you write it?

JLC: From my birth, it was ordained that I would approach writing a bit differently. I was born deaf to an all-Deaf family. My native language is ASL. I didn't begin to read until I was twelve years old. Until then, I always got poor grades in school. You probably know how it is in any branch of special education: They move you up the grades no matter what. I have old documents here stating that, in sixth grade, my English literacy was at the first grade level.

When I did start reading, though, it was a natural process picking up English. Unlike many deaf students who come from hearing families and who did not have *any* language until they went to school, I was fluent in a language. So it was only a matter of learning a second language.

In poetry, the first thing that is different for me is that I don't recognize rhymes or syllables. They don't exist to me. But one shouldn't assume that this means I wouldn't enjoy reading formal poetry. I have many favorites in traditional verse. I think that poems are often better when they are wrestled into place within a form—the very process of working and reworking the poems makes them stronger.

I do recognize line breaks. For me, they are about pausing and also suspending meaning. Take what James Wright wrote on a notepad to Donald Hall when Hall was visiting him in the hospital. Wright had throat cancer and could no longer speak, so he was writing notes like a deaf man. "Don, I'm dying," Wright wrote on one line, and paused before moving his pen to the next line, "for ice cream." I love it when poets use line breaks in that way, shifting the meaning, giving things double meanings.

Another thing that I recognize is repetition. When a poet repeats the same words in a poem, it does have what I think is a musical kind of effect on me.

When I wrote in large print, I sought out impromptu forms. Most often it would be using stanzas with the same number of lines. It's not a heavy line-by-line scheme, but it would still require some struggle. It would require me to rethink all sorts of things in different drafts before a poem comes to rest. Some poems would yield themselves better to two-line stanzas than to four-line stanzas. I would need to make sure each stanza made some sense as an unit unto itself, that each would help unfold the poem in meaningful ways.

When I started writing in Braille, stanzas no longer made much sense. Why? Because the Braille display shows only one line at a time. Sighted people can look at a page and know how long a poem is, that there's another stanza coming up. In Braille, I have no way of knowing if there is more. So each blank line at the end of a stanza could be, possibly, the end of the poem. I do go on to the next line to find out if there's more. Often I can tell that a poem is not finished, and I'd expect there to be more. Sometimes I'd think a poem is finished, and I'd think, Wow, what a great poem! Wait a minute! There's more. In such cases, I'd often be disappointed by what follows. One poet who does this to me more than any other is Billy Collins. I love his work, but many of his poems are one or two stanzas too long. I think he knows it. He told an interviewer that his wife helps him by telling him where a poem should stop, because he can run away with a poem.

It is logical, then, that I would abandon stanzas and also try not to go on too long in my poems. While I'm not particularly interested in line length, I do keep all of my lines within forty-four Braille characters. This is the length of my Braille display. When reading, I hate it when another poet's poem has lines going over this limit, requiring me to move to the "next" line which would only have a few words before the end of that line. This breaks up the experience of that line.

One last thing about Braille: It has many contractions, such as "rcv" being short for "receive" or a single character, "k," when standing alone, meaning "knowledge." This does influence certain word choices I make. Misreading print or typos have produced some famous poems, and my misreading or typos in Braille have given me happy accidents, too. For example, "quick" is "qk" in contracted Braille. The character "q" is one dot shy of the full cell of six dots. The full cell itself is short for "for" and consequently the word "quick" can feel like "fork." When I misread "quick-tempered" for a split second, I thought it was "fork-tempered." This, in turn, made me think of my mother. She has this way of being two things at once—indifferent and kind, or withholding and giving. Like being two people at once, having two heads, as if her personality is "forked." Soon I had a poem about her that used "fork-tempered"!

WG: Linda Pastan in a talk she gave at the last Dodge Poetry Festival made a point similar to the one you did about Billy Collins, saying that one common fault of poets is the tendency to continue a poem past the point when it should have stopped. How do you recognize when a poem you are writing has gone on too long? Can you lead us through an example of how you have had to revise a poem by making it shorter?

JLC: Yes, it's interesting that Linda Pastan has said a similar thing. I don't know what was said, but it might be worth nothing that I don't think Billy Collins goes *that* long. Collins wouldn't be Collins if he practiced Pastan's rigor or brevity. Collins is a talker; his poems *have* to do some talking. Cutting out too much of the talk would necessitate massive changes in his work. He'd end up like the hundreds of other poets who have cute ideas but misplace them in poems coiled too tight. Charm, after all, needs a dollop of excess. Poets like Pastan or me are not talkers and shouldn't aim for that kind of charm. We wouldn't do it right. We have to do what we can do right.

As for poems of mine that were short and needed to be expanded, you've asked the question wrong. There was only one poem that was too short. All of the others have been too long and required cutting.

Because of my writing process, it would be difficult to take you through a traditional play-by-play account of a poem's creation. You understand, I do most of the writing in my head. And often it wouldn't be in words but in the form of ideas. Those ideas have individual presences in my mental environment, like how people and objects exist in my physical one. An idea may have some words, some memories, and some of them are like experiences, as if I am living it, interacting with it.

I will try to take you inside a poem called "Thanksgiving." Not one of my best poems, but it's probably the clearest example. Now, my first idea was to give the reader a taste of my kind of music. Most people think that I'm missing out on something because I do not listen to music. The reality is that our world is full of phenomena, billions of stimuli swirling around us. It's only natural that we would recognize all sorts of patterns in this great flood. In fact, recognizing patterns is precisely how we become aware of anything at all. Equally natural is that certain patterns would please us more than others.

One thing that pleases me very much—don't laugh, or, better, go ahead and laugh and get it over with—is urinating into bottles. I discovered this pleasure on the road, of course. The roar of crashing waters against your palm, but without your hand getting wet. The heat of it, too, is sublime, not to mention the pleasure of urination itself. Different bottles are like different concert halls where the music would echo off the walls in different ways.

This seemed like a good idea for a poem. This idea included many things, such as phrases like "my kind of music" and saying something like "If you don't believe me, I'll sing / on you." That is, I would be putting people into my shoes by urinating on them—and in my mind, I became a reader, for some reason lying on the floor, and I experienced John Lee Clark, all six feet of him, towering over me, peeing on me. Weird, huh? You may be disappointed to read the poem after reading all of these interesting things, but it reads:

Thanksgiving

Traveling in the dark, we pull over for me
to piss into a bottle. Maple leaves
are burning somewhere in the distance. It fills
with warmth and the heft of my relief.

Yes, that's the whole of it. How did a cool idea for a naughty, more polemical poem become this whisper? I had every intention of going on to talk about "my kind of music" and leading things up to where I challenge the reader to believe me or else. But I couldn't. I'm not a talker like Billy Collins. In my hands, such a poem would be too cute, didactic, cheap. When I wrote the word "relief" I knew it had to stop there.

I like this poem, and I think it carries a lot of possibilities within its small space. It has many references to things that are in my world. "Thanksgiving": I love food, and when I eat I suppose I absorb more of the experience of gestation than do some people, as my eyes and ears are in my mouth. And it also means giving of thanks, and one of the things I am thankful for is relief. Then there's the nod to William Stafford's most famous poem, though he uses "through" whereas I use "in." I think "we pull over for me" is neat. It's not for me alone that we better pull over—my relief will be most acute to me, but others in the car would also be relieved. To not pull over would not only distress me; the tension would spread to everyone else. Then I didn't quite want the reader to be absolutely sure of what I'm doing with the bottle. The reader would have an idea, but I don't want the reader to put down her cup on the table yet. Instead of going directly to what happens to the bottle, I interrupt this logical step by introducing another source of pleasure, that scent of burning leaves in late fall. I suppose you could say that this is another instrument, and the two instruments join together in the end.

That's my reading, anyway. I didn't think of any of this in advance of writing the poem. I'm sure most readers will not think much about the poem. They'll just read, and it'll just be an experience. It doesn't matter what experience it is. Any would be valid. A yawn of boredom is commentary as important as a twenty-page analysis.

WG: I want to pick up on your statement that any experience that a reader had of your poem would be valid. Of course, in a certain tautological sense that is true, but I wonder if you also feel that any interpretations of that poem (or any of your poems) is equally valid. I have a hard time believing that even post-structuralists really believe that, but as an author I would think—assuming writing is more than therapy to you—you have certain expectations about the kind of response a poem might provoke and that given those responses you are going to feel that your poem is more or less successful. My question, I guess, is, as an artist, what kind of expectations do you have of your poems and how do you judge whether or not you have succeeded?

JLC: I believe that, as Sam Walton liked to say, the customer is always right. The reader is always right. When a reader dismisses me or any other poet after reading two or three words, she is right. Even if she dismisses a poem before reading it, she's right. Of course, I would like her to like my work, but I cannot expect that. After all, I can't stand most of the poetry I read.

The best I can do is to be aware of the great investment the reader is making when she picks up a poem of mine and deigns to read the title and the first few words. I try to make these few words pay. The first two lines should set up the poem or at least say something interesting. It's a mistake to open with a long series of adjectives or mere description. I also try to keep in mind the value each word carries. I think that verbs carry the most value and that adverbs carry the least. How apt it is that adverbs are called that—the negative opposite of verbs. Adverbs are to be avoided at almost any cost.

I hope this care on my part helps me succeed more often at returning the reader's investment. But the bottom line remains the same: I cannot expect anything. I have no right to. When I read, the only expectations that matter are my own. If any writer dares to argue with me outside of the text, I would be turned off. It's a blessing that the writer, as a physical person, doesn't exist when you read her work. I mean, the writer isn't there breathing down your neck, is she? If she was, I'm betting my last Helen Keller quarter that you wouldn't like it at all. The optimum reading experience is when you are free to throw the book away after the first sentence, or even before then. Not to say that you would, but if that freedom is there, you are also free to enjoy it, if it's worthy of your attention. This is why school isn't the place to cultivate readers. Students are not at full liberty. Only when it's OK that they don't read a single word do we have a proper reading environment.

WG: So you are saying that as a writer, you have absolutely no expectations at all of your poems? Given all of the work you put into a poem, that seems a little strange.

JLC: Yes, that's right. I have no expectations for my readers. I've explained that I do have expectations for myself when writing—trying to make the first few words do their job, use words with carrying power instead of words that detract from the power of the poem. But no matter how much work I put into a poem, no reader is under any obligation to even glance at it.

If someone likes Apple better than Microsoft, that's the end of the matter. At that moment, anyway. Microsoft can run around crying, "But we spent $6 billion in research and development on this! Don't you know you can have more games with us than with them?" That wouldn't change anything. If a movie is a flop at the box office, that's that. How many years the studio put into the movie doesn't change a single thing. The product failed, period.

Things are more complicated than that, of course. Readers have different tastes, for example. Poets have different styles, things they can do well and things they can't do well. Still, the fact is that when a poem is written, it's a product and it's on its own. Marketing can help bring people to it, but whether they stay to read or not still depends on the text. There are expectations, as certain elements can buy more of the reader's attention. One such case is Sylvia Plath. Her tragic story enhances her following. If she had lived to a good old age, she would still have been a great poet, but she wouldn't have the same following.

Another element that can buy more of some readers' interest or patience is the Helen Keller Card. The poet is a little boy dying of cancer, for example. Even if his poems are no good, they can get a lot of attention. As a DeafBlind poet, I'm aware that some readers come to my work for the "wrong" reasons. Instead of fighting against this, I work with it in the hope that they will soon have better reasons to like my work and to recommend it. Don't get me wrong. It isn't all right to exploit a poet's disability for the sake of marketing alone. But the Helen Keller Card can be and should be used as part of a larger marketing strategy, the most important part of which should be the quality of the poet's work.

When I produce a poem I think is very good, I do have faith in it. Take "My Understanding One Day of Foxgloves." After writing it, I thought it was one of my best poems. Excited, I sent it to a dozen magazines. All rejected it. They were mid-level venues. I then send it to places down the food chain. More rejections. On a lark, I decided to send it to the top, to *Poetry* magazine. Well, what do you know—they accepted it. I was tempted to go to all those places that rejected it and tell them how wrong they were.

Since that time, however, I have come to appreciate that all of those rejections were just as valid as the acceptance. In fact, I now agree with what one editor said about my poem when he rejected it. They were not wrong to reject it. They were just doing their job. And I was just doing my job, having faith in my work and giving them the chances they need. Poets are often surprised by what their readers love the most. All I can do is write, try my best, and send my poems off to be on their own.

WG: I'm sure that as a poet with a disability, you face some challenges in doing readings that not every poet faces. Will you talk about those?

JLC: For Deaf poets, giving a reading presents a peculiar mixture of problems. Aesthetically, there is the question of how to read their poems in public. Although some can speak, many don't feel comfortable using their nasal, broken speech in public. Others, like me, do not speak at all. Signing, then, is a strong preference. However, it's not easy to translate one's own written poems into ASL that is also ASL poetry. A Deaf poet is not necessarily an ASL poet. Many are not even native signers, and would feel equally awkward signing poems in public. If they can only sign pidgin versions that would not be very pleasing to Deaf audience members and if the hearing audience members are listening to an interpreter reading the written poems while they gape at the signing Deaf poet, what's the point of the reading?

Still, I'm sure that Deaf poets would be able to resolve such aesthetic issues if they had more opportunities. They could, for example, enlist the help of an ASL poet in producing rich, full translations and be coached in the art of sign performance. But there's a practical problem that has long limited Deaf poets' opportunities to do readings: Interpreting costs. This same issue also means there are very few literary events that are accessible to Deaf people. In most parts of the country, interpreting services start at $120, which covers the first two hours and is required even if you only need one hour or fifteen minutes. So it's automatically $120, and sixty dollars per hour after the first two hours. This effectively excludes bookstores, for the costs would blow away any sales. The great bulk of other readings are hosted by small organizations with little or no money. This leaves the larger organizations and colleges which could handle the costs, in theory if not in practice.

It's no wonder only two Deaf poets in my anthology have given more than one reading. A few, myself included, have given just one. The rest have never had the privilege. While this is a sore spot for some, I and some others are fine with it. Why? Because, at heart, poetry readings are a hearing thing. The whole point, after all, is to hear the poet reading her work. I've attended some and have never enjoyed them, because most of what the interpreter is trying to sign makes no sense. It's much better to stay at home and read the poet's work. Since most people at a hearing poet's reading would be hearing non-signers, it's not a social event I'd enjoy either.

As a DeafBlind person who listens to ASL tactilely, the practical side is different. Standard practice requires that there be two interpreters for a tactile listener. They would switch places every twenty minutes. This means $240 to start with. This further diminishes my opportunities to do readings. Because I am a native signer, though, the aesthetic side is easier. In the end, the greatest problem is cultural. Unless there are Deaf people involved, such as the person who picks me up at the airport being Deaf or a signer and there being Deaf people in the audience with whom I can socialize afterwards, I would be hard pressed to accept an invitation to read. I'd feel like a stranger in a strange land asked to perform a foreign custom.

WG: As a native ASL speaker, if you wanted to translate one of your written poems into ASL (or translate an ASL poem into written English), what would be some of the aesthetic considerations for you? In *Deaf American Poetry* you discuss Clayton Valli's original reluctance to let Raymond Luczak translate his poem "A Dandelion" from ASL into English. Knowing what

Luczak came up with, do you think Valli was right in being leery of the translation? If you translate one of your English poems to ASL do you consider it a completely different poem?

JLC: Some ASL poets remain skeptical of translation. After all, some don't know English well, let alone English poetry. The most beautiful English poem in the world would mean nothing. It can be hard for some to imagine how it's possible for those stupid fancy words to convey what they sign. Also, many of the pioneering ASL poets taught ASL and linguistics for a living and were engaged in academic battles against mainstream linguists who were not yet convinced of ASL's status as an actual language. So they may have felt protective of their ASL poems, preferring that one know ASL first before having any access to their work.

Now that ASL is widely recognized as a legitimate language, some ASL poets are growing more practical about their work and agreeing to have it voiced, glossed, or translated. I'm slowly working on getting more poets to allow me or others to translate their work. It may take five more years before we have a full-length collection of translations of ASL poetry.

I think the way I approach translation is the same way most translators do: Crumple the original poem into a tiny wad, chew it for a while, spit it out, unwrap it, try to pat it down as flat and neat as possible. Because ASL grammar is quite different, though, the process may be more like translating between English and Chinese than between two Romance languages. ASL's basic grammatical structure is topic-comment. Sometimes this means short, contained passages are object-subject-verb/adjective. Instead of "That's a beautiful blue car" it is essential in ASL to start with the topic, which is the car, and then comment on it: CAR THERE BLUE THAT WOW BEAUTIFUL.

The "there" is important for placing the car somewhere in the spatial signing space. The next time the car is referred to, it will appear in the same "place" as would things and characters in movies. If the hero looks to the left of the screen and the heroine in the other direction, they stay that way throughout the scene if not the whole movie. This helps to orient the viewer. We do the same in ASL. If I'm recounting a conversation I had with my six-year-old son, I would look down to the right as if talking to my son, and when I quote my son, I'd be looking up to the left to reflect the way he looked up to me during that conversation. In my recounting, I create a short film in which I play both myself and my son. The challenge in translating this is to create equally clear and consistent switches between people and things, what they are like or doing. Fortunately, there are nifty tricks in English that accomplish all these things, though not in a literally cinematic way. When translating from English to ASL, I often have to start with something later in the original poem because it offers the best point of entry, that is, the topic. Otherwise, the descriptions would mean nothing in ASL. The thunderstorm, the winds, the crashing sea would mean nothing without first knowing there's a house on a cliff. In English, it may be all right to hold the house until later, but not in ASL. If the English depends too much on the house being held back, it's possible that the ASL version wouldn't be a good poem. That can happen. Sometimes, it's not worth it. But if the English poem has other sources of power, it shouldn't be a problem to start with the house and make up for the rearrangement somewhere else.

Some of my poems in English I haven't bothered translating. It *could* be done, but the best possible result in ASL wouldn't be worth performing to a Deaf audience. The best translations come from poems that lend themselves readily to sets of similar handshapes or a visual space that has a pattern in it that distinguishes it as ASL poetry. For example, my poem "Long Goodbyes" plays with the idea of time and is about Deaf people talking around the table in the kitchen, which is the most important place in Deaf culture. When Deaf friends come, they stay forever around the table, chatting for hours and hours before anyone stands up to go. When everyone stands up, it will take hours yet before they actually leave. The sign "hour" is the index finger as the hour hand going around the face of an imaginary clock, and the table is round too, and the Deaf people, whether they are sitting or standing, stay in a constant circle. So a pattern emerges for the ASL version in which the circle as a shape plays a prominent role. This influences how I choose to sign other things, all toward the circular motion of signing hands and the passing of time.

Are the versions completely different? No. That one is on paper and the other signed would give the illusion that they are. But if someone translated my ASL version back into English, the skeleton should be there, maybe some meat. But the skin and hair and the clothes would probably be different. For example,

I doubt that the line "light to light bright in the night" would reappear, because this is more of an English flourish. It would disappear in the ASL version. In its stead is an ASL flourish in which the two hands signing the flashing of light segues into an innovative doubled sign for "night" that happens to be circular in shape. As different as the two flourishes are, they don't alter the skeleton at all. They're just flourishes.

WG: John, I think that the whole process of translating is fascinating to put in general and really appreciate the window that you have provided into how this works with ASL. Obviously, there are many more areas that we could go into from here, but as a practical matter, we need to wrap things up. My last question to you is: What advice would you give to aspiring disabled poets?

JLC: My first piece of advice to any aspiring poet would be to read. It's shocking how many aspire to write who don't read much at all. The result of this is simple: They will not write well. I love what Raymond Luczak has said many times: "You write what you read."

This saying may be repulsive to a young poet who wants to be a rebel, who wants to write "original" poetry. I know that I feared influence when I started out. I didn't want to be influenced; I wanted to be my own man. What I didn't realize at that time was that influence is food. Without it, my writing starved and stank. You are what you eat.

It took me years to realize that reading and being open to influence wouldn't mean I would be a copycat. Instead, it's a complex, organic process like digestion. Eating nothing but pizza for a month wouldn't mean I would have cheese for my skin and tomato sauce in my veins. But it would certainly mean growing very fat and pushing my heart thirty years closer to a heart attack. Conversely, eating vegetables for a month wouldn't mean I'd turn green. I'd still be me, but my health would be much better. Reading is vital to the health of my writing.

My next bit of advice is to submit your work. And I mean submit. Submit everywhere, all the time. I began submitting my work right away, even if my work was crap. Reading *Poet's Market*, submitting, and getting rejected taught me more than years of classes would have. Aside from the practical bits about the business side of writing, I learned to become detached from my poems. Putting them through the machinery of submissions helped me appreciate them for what they are: products. I would still love them, but in a different way, respectful of their limitations, of their small place in the entertainment business.

Something must be dead to me before I can bring it back to life in poetry. If it's still alive, the art is compromised. When I started writing poems, they were about things still alive to me and so they were poor poems. Submitting them mechanically taught me to let things die. First, it taught me to let go of the poems in the first place. When they were rejected, I learned to let go of the poems in another way. Later, I was letting go as I wrote. Now, the subject of my next poem is already dead, making my job as embalmer much easier.

For disabled poets, my best advice is to write about disability. Or, rather, let disability, as part of your life, appear in your work. Disability is everywhere. It is, in fact, universal, for to be human is to be disabled. The only reason some people don't think of themselves as disabled is because most things out there are designed to accommodate their type of body and not other types.

No matter how disabled people are marginalized, disability has influenced all human history, and its place in society today is as unavoidable as ever. Since disabled poets are going to influence society anyway, they might as well make it an honest exercise. I know many disabled writers who don't write about disability at all. I think they are making a great mistake. There's space for them, and society cannot help but respond in some way, and they use this power to . . . write "mainstream" fare?

It's sad that it's even called a "choice" to write about one's disability. I never consciously chose to write about my Deaf upbringing or DeafBlind culture. I just write, and my deafness, my blindness, my life just flows out.

So there you go: Read, submit, and embrace disability in your work.

A QUESTION THAT'S HARDER THAN IT SHOULD BE

These past couple of months I have been grappling with a question. Should I stop submitting my poems to magazines I don't have access to? The answer should be simple. I mean, who wants to appear in a venue that excludes him? Why support something that discriminates against you?

It is the latest in a long series of questions I've asked myself as a DeafBlind writer. When I first began submitting my work to literary journals twelve years ago, I read books with a CC-TV, which enlarged the letters and had them in white against a black background. One of the most frequent visitors to the rolling table under my CC-TV was *Poet's Market*. I must have submitted to 90 percent of the magazines listed. I spent so much time with the 2003 edition that I assembled a found poem called "Advice to Poets" drawn from editors' comments in the book.

Then it became harder and harder to read with my eyes. I had been reading Braille for years, and I always brought Braille books when I traveled, the CC-TV being too heavy to lug around. But it wasn't until 2006 that the State Services for the Blind finally agreed to get me a Braille display for my computer. It was one of the most liberating moments in my life.

However, I found that this meant some changes in how I handled the business side of my writing. Because producing addressed envelopes was such a hassle, I decided to submit my work by e-mail only. Loath to stop sending work to certain magazines, I wrote to them, asking if they would be willing to accommodate me by considering e-mail submissions from me. Most of the editors were gracious and said yes. A few, though, weren't so nice. I never sent work to those again.

All was well for a while. Then I noticed that some editors forgot to respond to my submissions. Since I had submitted work in a different way, it was understandable, my falling through the cracks. It was also becoming tiresome, having to ask for an accommodation first. And wasn't there an ethical issue here?

What about other writers like me? Shouldn't all magazines at least have a provision already in place for writers unable to use surface mail? I decided to stop sending work to magazines that did not accept e-mail submissions.

Fortunately, magazines began adopting online submission systems. It is a joy to use those online submission forms, and I've mastered this process to such a degree I can do it in my sleep. While I missed being able to submit to *any* magazine, there were hundreds upon hundreds that I could send my work to.

As I began to appear in some of those magazines, I was disturbed by the fact I couldn't always enjoy reading the issues I was in. It is possible to scan a magazine and then save the text file, which I could read via my computer and Braille display. But this doesn't work well with poetry, because the scanning program disregards line breaks. It was frustrating trying to read fellow poets' contributions. I gave up reading any print journals. (*Poetry* magazine is the only poetry publication available in hard-copy Braille. For this reason, I often send my work to them first, even if that sometimes works against me. I can get too excited and send off new poems before they're cooked.)

That's how I got to wondering about whether or not I should limit myself to online journals and print journals that have significant online archives. I love that there are so many online journals that are easy for me to read. Not all of them are accessible—some use fancy image links that pose a barrier, some rely on PDFs that my screen-reading software cannot process—but many of them are. When I appeared in a few, I was so happy to share them with my blind and DeafBlind friends, knowing that they would have access to my work.

So what's the problem? Isn't the solution simple? Just submit to the accessible venues.

Well, as a poet, I don't respect all of the online journals. The quality of some, to be frank, embarrasses me. There are fine ones, but there are more print journals that publish high-octane work. I've made something of a career out of my poetry, winning grants and fellowships. I believe that the fact I've appeared in some of the most prestigious places has helped me earn this recognition. Whereas I once had the entire *Poet's Market* at my disposal, I now have less than half of the field to play in. I've been steadily blacklisting magazines—first those magazines that had a bad attitude about my asking them for accommodations, then those that don't accept e-mail or online submissions, and now I'm going to delete even more names from my book?

Principle or prestige?

Since I don't know for sure if sending work only to the journals I have access to will have a negative effect on my career, I am going to try the principled route. I'll be able to enjoy reading the issues I'm in. I'll be able to pass the links along to my friends with a clean conscience. As for the grants and fellowships, I shouldn't be worried. What matters is that I write the best work I can write, right? I hope that's the case.

ASL LITERATURE ON PAPER

For a long time, I have been bothered by the lack of growth in ASL literature. Why aren't there more stories and poems? Why are there so few ASL creators following in the steps of pioneers such as Clayton Valli? Why aren't there ASL novels? And, most troubling of all, why aren't more people lapping up the literature that we do have? I've met too many people who shrug and say, "Not interested."

I had vague ideas as to why, but when I learned about recent developments in written ASL, everything became clear to me.

There have been earlier attempts at a written system. They fall into two categories: illustration and notation. Sutton's SignWriting is a good example of the former, as it includes the whole upper body. Head, arms, hands, torso. Line after line of mannequins with their limbs in different positions. Stokoe's system of recording ASL words by using Roman letters and Arabic numerals belongs to the latter group. But the new development is the first that feels like *reading*, not deciphering, and *writing*, as opposed to drawing or writing in code.

The new approach, which has already split into several camps, with my favorite being the ASLwrite group, uses only the strokes necessary to establish the words, nothing more. Extramanual markers, such as facial expressions, are added only when necessary for clear composition or to distinguish between potentially different meanings. In spite of this stripped-down approach, it is still faithful enough to actual signing that an ASL student can learn it and can read a new ASL word, one she has never seen spoken before, and know how to say it. Add the fact that people who already know ASL can become fluent in written ASL in a matter of weeks, and we have here the strongest claim ever for there being a written form of ASL.

What does it mean for ASL literature? It solves the fundamental problems that have held ASL literature back for centuries. The first problem has to do with how participation in creating ASL literature has not been open and accessible to everyone in the signing community.

It's no accident that most of the pioneers in ASL literature were actors. They were trained as performers, to express clear ASL, to follow scripts. Feeling at home onstage or in front of cameras, the artistic ones found themselves experimenting and creating with their hands. Also, Hollywood and Broadway weren't clamoring for Deaf actors. Becoming a storyteller (Bernard Bragg), a comedian (Mary Beth Miller), or a poet (Patrick Graybill) was a way to remain onstage as much as possible.

Meanwhile, a few others who were not actors by trade also experimented and created (such as Ella Mae Lentz and Valli). To share their work, however, they had to become performers. It might have been possible for a non-performer to create ASL pieces and have a professional performer execute them. But the logistics necessary to pull this off were such that they effectively prevented anyone from doing this in any notable way until Valli's second video poetry collection. By then, he was an established figure in the community and had special access to video equipment and performers (most of whom were his students).

There were also a few Deaf writers writing in English. They had to grapple with the oppressive weight of the canon's long tradition of audism. It took a long time before the first novel by a Deaf American about the Deaf community was written—Douglass Bullard's *Islay* (1986).

There were an unknown number of Deaf people who possessed the gift of wit, observation, and artistic synthesis but who, for whatever reasons, could not or would not become performers or write at length in English. Such hidden gems shared casual stories with friends, told the wickedest jokes at the club, and burst out in poetic eloquence at meetings or at the kitchen table. My father is one of them, a born poet, the creator of many sparkling fragments he's not inclined to "perform" on purpose. These moments of clairvoyance and literary brilliance were not harnessed nor built upon.

While literature in ASL can escape the weight of the English canon more effectively than deaf literature in English can, it has serious challenges of its own. One is that the ASL speaker doesn't have the same advantages that a writer enjoys. The hearing critic Arthur Krystal dwelt on these advantages in a *New York Times* essay called "When Writers Speak." He noticed how writers he admired didn't sound as smart when they spoke. He understood, because he feels smarter when he himself writes. Perhaps writers don't think until they sit down to write!

When Krystal discussed this with the Harvard psychologist Steven Pinker, the latter suggested a more precise way of explaining this phenomenon. As Krystal rephrased it, Pinker pointed out that "the reason we sound smarter when writing is because we deliberately set out to be clear and precise, a luxury not usually afforded us in conversation." This explanation bears on spoken ASL, for its speakers usually have only conversational literacy in their language. Without writing the words on paper, they have almost no opportunity to study what they're saying, to go back and revise, or to mull for a moment over how to put something before saying it.

Another challenge is that it can be easy for performer and viewer alike to treat ASL literature like eye candy. ASL is so visually elastic that many creators fall in love with its cinematic qualities, focusing on those at the expense of content. But, always, after a while the special effects start to become cloying. Performers become frustrated, and viewers lose interest until the next novelty act arrives on the scene. Few realize that the core problem is that the story itself isn't strong—poor character development, no plot, lack of conflict, no emotional payoff.

But when a story is written down on paper, it is naked. Written ASL will, as written English does, force authors to inject narrative power or literary beauty into the very text. And when a performer with dynamite hands tells the story, it will work because the story already worked just fine without the performer. Content is the boss.

It makes sense that these historical challenges has limited the creation of high-quality ASL literature. The signing community, like all of the cultures that do not have or did not have a written language, has a rich tradition of passing stories down through the generations. As important as this tradition is, it doesn't function in the same way that literature does. Literature is the ever-changing DNA of the community, representing in meaningful and memorable forms the lives and experiences of a people. Deaf writers in English and ASL performers do contribute to this literature, but there are huge gaps. To fill these, we need to have ASL writers sitting at their desks late at night, poring over and tinkering with the fifth draft of a novel.

We know why we don't yet have an ASL novel. To create such a sophisticated, sustained work would be extremely difficult with only conversational, on-the-spot-and-then-gone ASL at our disposal. But even if someone managed to cobble together a DVD novel made up of a long series of "chapters," performed and taped one at a time, it's not likely that it would have been a success. While I loved Bernard Bragg's box-set video memoir *The Man Behind the Mask*, it didn't sell as well as his book *Lessons in Laughter*, co-written with Eugene Bergman. Ben Bahan's fable *Bird of a Different Feather* was superbly done, but I had trouble keeping my attention trained on the screen after the first five minutes. Similarly, Patrick Graybill's extended ASL summary of Harlan Lane's monumental history *When the Mind Hears* was a flop. Graybill is always a joy to watch, such an exquisite speaker, but the product as a whole did not work. Why?

Because of what I call the movie problem. You know how people always say that the book is better than the movie? No matter how good the movie is, there's nothing like entering into a book. One cannot enter the movie; the screen is always at some remove. The story, in the movie, is happening to other people. But in the book, you are *there*. The story is happening to you. The movie has decided how everyone looks, and it's never as you would have imagined it.

This problem is the same reason the blind community has a literacy issue. Most blind children go to public schools where their teachers know nothing about Braille. This means most blind people rely exclusively on audio materials. They may speak English well and they may have unlimited exposure to spoken English, but they are not fully literate in English. They still need Braille. Carl T. Rodgers explains in *Understanding Braille*: "The benefits inherent in direct visual or tactual reading experiences cannot be replaced by listening to the printed word through someone else's voice."

Someone else's voice. Someone else's hands. It's not that we cannot enjoy ASL performances. Readings, videos, and theater are still important. But there's something about the abstract, bare symbols on the page that invites our minds to engage, argue with, and absorb the language before us. We cannot do these things as well when we are only spectators.

One of the most important things the new developers did with written ASL was to make it a rule that writers are to project themselves spatially onto the page. If the writer is right-handed and says "Hello," his hand, from his own point of view, moves right. He is to write "Hello" in that way. He is *not* to write as if it's someone else saying "Hello" to him. Written ASL does not create a movie screen or a line of mannequins. Instead, it creates space for us to say things as ourselves. And it creates space, when we are reading it, to fall into the text. In that space, we are *there*.

And that's how ASL literature will finally get there, too.

ON
MY DEAFBLIND EXPERIENCE

SKYWAYS

I'm sure there are many who say they love Saint Paul more than any other place on earth, but for me to say that would be an understatement. That's because living anywhere outside of downtown Saint Paul would be like being in jail. I live in the heart of the skyway system in downtown, and for me it is freedom. You see, I am both Deaf and blind.

Many DeafBlind Americans live within invisible prison walls. No, it's not because of DeafBlindness itself, but because many places don't have the transportation, services, and access that would make it possible to be independent without hearing and sight. So, in many places, DeafBlind people feel stuck, just as anyone without legs would feel stuck if there's no wheelchair and there are no sidewalks outside. But Saint Paul isn't one of those bad places for people with slightly different bodies. Minnesota has some of the nation's best transportation services and other apparatus for accessibility.

The skyway system, though, is the frosting on the cake. It is so much easier to get around through skyways than crossing streets. It is not safe for me to cross a street on my own, so to do that, I hold up a card and hope someone will come along soon, see it, read it, and then offer to guide me across. That works, and I do that if I am traveling beyond the skyways. But it's so wonderful when I don't need to hold up that card and wait in the cold.

Thanks to the skyways, I can experience the same ease that most people do. Most things out there are designed for people's convenience, but they're for hearing and sighted people. If you feel like coffee, you can drive to the nearest coffee shop. And that's going to be very near you from anywhere you may be coming. But many of my fellow DeafBlind citizens don't have that privilege. They have to call paratransit to book a ride three days in advance—imagine how bad their hankering for that mocha latte must be by then! But I can just up and go. Just elevator down to the skyway level and then tap the tip of my white cane on the variously textured surfaces through different buildings.

After living here for five years, I know downtown Saint Paul like the back of my hand. But the landscape in my mind is very different from what you might see and store in your mind. I wouldn't be surprised that there are many ugly sights, such as all those bland logos of fast food chains. Perhaps the skyways feel claustrophobic to some, and to others they may be just another gray patch of corporate America. But for me, they're more than pure beauty. They're freedom.

UNREASONABLE EFFORT

Being Deaf and blind, it's not uncommon for me to encounter awe in others. It doesn't take much to impress them, since their expectations for what a DeafBlind person can do are so low. But I have friends and colleagues who are more aware and are able to appreciate my accomplishments as the natural result of my talents. However, they can still be surprised—by my lack of a college degree.

Oh yes, I did go to college and on scholarship too. But my three attempts at formal higher education over a decade all failed.

No, this failure is not due to DeafBlindness. DeafBlind people can do anything. The question is not whether or not we can or should do something, but *how* we are going to do it. Being DeafBlind, in and of itself, is never the problem; the problem lies elsewhere, in lack of access, in bigotry and ignorance, in narrow rules and definitions that discriminate against and exclude us. DeafBlind people are capable of gaining knowledge, thinking critically, and synthesizing and applying information and thought.

Yet only a handful of DeafBlind people have graduated from college. Because the leading cause of DeafBlindness—Usher syndrome—is a progressive condition, there are many DeafBlind people who hold degrees that they obtained while they still had the use of hearing or sight. Going to college fully deaf and blind is another story.

How did those few succeed in college? Almost all of them had full-time companions who can be described as their co-students. It was a team effort going beyond the mere utilization of the companion's eyes and ears and interpreting services. Helen Keller, the first DeafBlind person to graduate from college, had Anne Sullivan Macy. Robert J. Smithdas, the second person to do so half a century later, had John Singer (who was literally a co-student, registered and all). Mae Brown, the first one in Canada, twenty years after, had Joan MacTavish.

An illuminating note: MacTavish would later pioneer the training and professionalization of intervenors—or support service providers as they are called in the United States or communication guides as they are known elsewhere—and this role now has a code of conduct and rules to guide both parties. But, MacTavish confessed in her biography of Mae Brown, "I cannot see Mae and I succeeding if we had been obliged to work within [the code of professional conduct]. As a team, we worked equally."

Such collaborations have become unacceptable, not only to the increasingly empowered DeafBlind community, but also to institutions of higher education. Disability rights legislation requires schools to provide disabled students with "reasonable accommodations" while absolving schools of anything they may argue as an "undue burden." For DeafBlind students, reasonable accommodations may include ASL interpreters for classroom sessions, notetakers, certain equipment, and transcription of textbooks into Braille. One would think that, given all these wonderful services, DeafBlind students would be more successful in college today. Why is this not the case?

Because traditional schooling at the college level is biased against Braille readers. There is a reason why almost all hearing blind students rely almost exclusively on audio books and readers, even if they prefer Braille. Audio reading is slower than reading by sight, so hearing blind students do find themselves working harder. Braille reading is even slower, meaning DeafBlind students have to spend three to five times as many hours as other students to read the same materials. Using signing readers is a poor alternative, not only because it is equally slow but because there will be much lost in translation, leaving the student underequipped to write good papers based on the language of the readings.

Slow reading shouldn't be made into a disadvantage. I have found that it helps me absorb what I read at a deeper level. I remember more and retain it longer. I am often dismayed by how little others read into what they sweep through with their eyes. Reading slowly is a big reason why I had no trouble writing great papers.

But I have never been able to hand in all the due papers. I always got behind in reading. I would either submit my assignment late and swallow the automatic grade drop or skip it altogether, so I could read in advance for the next assignment in hopes of making it on time for that one. No matter how much my professors raved about my work, the controlling factor is whether or not a student completes everything, however poorly. And being granted more time doesn't really work, because I would have new classes or be forced to not sign up for any, or for only one or two per term.

Doing coursework and gaining an education are two different things. Helen Keller, Robert J. Smithdas, and Mae Brown all took exams without their companions. What they demonstrated by passing them was that they learned what they were supposed to learn. But it is doubtful that they would have fulfilled all the course requirements in the time they did without the help or, to put it more accurately, the active participation of their co-students.

That a good chunk of traditional schooling involves meaningless hoops for students to jump through is well known and much lamented by educators who care about genuine learning. But such things are put up with because they make it possible for schools to process large numbers of students in the classic capitalist manner. Almost all the curricula and syllabi are streamlined around the assumption that students are hearing and sighted and can read at a certain speed. Schools are navigable for most students. But for DeafBlind students, they are nearly impossible.

Nearly. There are a few DeafBlind students today who are managing. To be one of them, one must meet a set of qualifications. One must be brilliant. One must be extraordinarily driven. One must have no social life or responsibilities outside of school. And one must be prepared to sacrifice many more years than what is required of most students. There may be reasonable accommodations, but those DeafBlind students must put in unreasonable effort.

This is a troubling picture. In the background, there are dim-witted students with lukewarm ambitions who hold down part-time jobs and party all the while making faster progress toward graduation. I may be blind, but I can see a bad deal. Since I had aspirations that would benefit from my having advanced degrees, I thought I could sustain the losses in such a lopsided arrangement. After three attempts that produced no tangible gains, however, I have learned that some things just aren't worth it. Still, I would like something to be done about higher education for DeafBlind students.

We live in a society obsessed with credentials, and that has to change. It is not right for any group of people to be so effectively barred from earning them. But it's also wrong for employers to take advantage of this. They should invest in evaluating each applicant's true qualifications.

For their part, institutions of higher education have a responsibility to all communities and populations. If someone is capable of learning, accessible and effective resources must be made available. If someone gains knowledge and expertise, proper recognition is due. Reasonable effort must be rewarded with equal credit.

An ideal educational system for DeafBlind students does not demand unreasonable accommodations or concessions. It demands a return to the roots of higher education, where quality takes precedence over quantity and true learning and facility over mere schooling. The problems in education that DeafBlind students expose affect everyone else, so the solutions wouldn't be for DeafBlind students only. They would benefit everyone.

MY DADDY

As part of our mentorship workshop with the esteemed Japanese-American author David Mura, the five 2011 Beyond the Pure Fellows were asked to write a sketch of ourselves. We were encouraged to do so in the third person. Here, I imagined what one of my sons might say if asked to describe his father.

Daddy is really, really strong. He can lift my whole weight with one hand, one finger almost. This is very good because we can have lots of fun! I love it when he swings me round and round and I'm laughing so hard. I know he gets tired after a while, but I can't help it. We always say, "Again! Again!" Bebe is heavier than I am, so he always goes first, because Daddy says it's easier to go from heavy to lighter than lighter to heavy. But Daddy is always fair. If Bebe gets another turn after me, I get another turn, too.

And Daddy always brings candy and cookies. That's because he goes food shopping most of the time, not Mommy. Three times a week either his friend Rocky or Dawn picks him up. He says they are his friends, but that's not why they come to pick him up. They are paid to drive him to wherever he wants to go and tell him what they see. I went with Daddy a few times, and he goes really fast. He knows where everything is. When he's not sure which jar on the shelf is the kind he wants, he asks Rocky or Dawn. If there are any sales, Rocky or Dawn will tell Daddy and he will think about it. When Mommy goes food shopping, she doesn't bring back candy or cookies, or only a little. I think Daddy buys more candy and cookies because he likes them too.

I love throwing the football with Daddy. He can throw it really, really far. So he waits to make sure I'm far enough straight ahead of him. Then he throws it. Sometimes I catch it. Sometimes not. Then I run closer to where Daddy is standing. I try to hit him with the football. If I hit him, he catches it most of the time. It doesn't hurt him because it's a Nerf football. If I miss, he walks near it and moves his cane to find it. I've asked him many times how he knows where the football is if he can't see it. He always says he felt it thump on the grass and he knew where it went. But I still can't understand how he can find it.

Mommy can see most of the time. But sometimes she doesn't see what I am saying, so I put my hands under her hands, like I do with Daddy. Then I know for sure Mommy saw what I was saying. Like yesterday, when I asked her for cookies. She said no, not now. So I put my hands under hers and said, "Cookies!" She laughed and gave me one.

I love it when Daddy tells us stories. Like The Three Pigs, but the straws are free, from McDonald's. And then Lincoln Logs. Then the Legos one. I like Legos and we have a big, BIG box of Legos. The wolf is in a suit because he's the banker. And there's the story about the lumberjack. The way Mommy tells it, one of the trees is deaf. So the lumberjack has to spell T-I-M-B-E-R to make the tree fall down. The way Daddy tells it, the tree is deaf and blind. So the lumberjack has to climb up and spell "timber" under a leaf. Whoosh! The tree falls down WITH the lumberjack! The best story of all is the gum story. Daddy is so funny when he plays the man, the jogger, the old lady, and BOTH the boyfriend and the girlfriend at the SAME time!

Daddy reads all the time. Everywhere. In the car, in bed, and even when he goes potty. His books are BIG. Mommy's books are small and have the words in them. Daddy's books have tiny bumps in them. Mommy draws really, really good cartoons, just like in the newspapers. Daddy writes. Mommy drew two books, and Daddy has two books too. I think I want to do both when I grow up! Then I'll have FOUR books!

ALL THAT I CAN'T LEAVE BEHIND

You notice a young man sitting on a park bench with a large book on his lap, his fingers flying over its pages. The white cane leaning against the bench confirms your idea that he is blind. You turn to the hot dog stand and order a chili dog. Turning back to look at the bench, you see that he's gone. Lying on the bench is the large book, a couple of its pages fluttering in the wind. Scanning around, you spy the blind man walking briskly a block away. If history is any indication, you will drop your chili dog, grab the book, and run after him like you have never run before in your life.

How I wish I could get rid of magazines—for it was a Braille magazine, not a book, that I left on the bench—as easily as the sighted do. They can cast aside an issue anywhere and go on with their lives. Not so with me.

I receive half a dozen magazines every month from the National Library Services for the Blind and Physically Handicapped. A Braille reader can "subscribe" to any number of magazines from their list for free. If one borrows books from the library, they have to be returned, just like print library books. But the magazines are different. They are not to be returned. They are yours to keep or throw away.

At home, I throw them in the recycling bin. But when I'm traveling, I don't want to lug those bulky editions around with me after I'm done reading them. So I shed them as I go along, or I try to. At a restaurant, I might finish an issue and leave it behind after paying the bill and before walking out. More often than not, however, a waiter will overtake me, panting, and press the Braille magazine into my hands. I am then forced to smile in gratitude. After walking a safe distance, I will begin to look for a garbage can.

But even that doesn't always work. I have thrust magazines deep in trash cans only to have them, dripping with garbage goo, presented to me a few minutes later. On account of magazines I've discarded, people have run, jumped into cars, tripped over themselves, called, mailed, asked a mutual acquaintance to please pass them on to me, or saved them for weeks until, finally seeing me again, rushing up to me. "There you are! You forgot this last time you were here." How could I tell them the truth?

Because blind people do many things a bit differently, I suppose it's not easy for sighted people to realize that we know exactly what we are doing. The strong temptation is to assume that we've made a mistake or misplaced our things and that we need help. That we do sometimes need assistance—for which we can and will ask—muddles the image we wish to promote. What are we to do but smile and say, "Thank you"?

Last week, I flew out East to give a lecture on DeafBlind history at the University of Virginia. In addition to my backpack, I carried a bag with eight magazine volumes. I succeeded in hiding one of them, after finishing it, in the seat pocket in front of me before I disembarked in Philadelphia, where my connecting flight was. I hid another one in the same way on the plane that landed in Charlottesville. So far, so good.

I didn't have much time to read during the excitement of my stay in town, but I did finish two more volumes by the time Professor Christopher Krentz picked me up from the hotel to take me to the airport. Before checking out, I decided to just leave those two volumes in my room, rather than look for a garbage can in the hotel big enough to bury them in. But to be safe, I tore them up. That would make it clear that they were to be thrown away.

By the time I landed back at the Minneapolis/St. Paul airport, I had read through the last four magazine volumes. I hid one of them on the plane, but felt it too risky to hide the other three in three more seat pockets. On my way to the where the taxis were, I stepped into a restroom, used it, and right before exiting, I abandoned the last three issues. Fearing that they might come back to haunt me, I walked at a smart, almost dangerous clip, my cane zipping back and forth in front of me. No one caught up with me. I got into a taxi and I was home safe!

Or so I thought. Waiting in my inbox at home was an email message from the hotel manager saying he had my "books." Would I please give him my address so he could mail them to me?

JOHNNY WAKES UP

On a discussion list of professionals, many of whom were vocational rehabilitation counselors, serving the DeafBlind community, the question of whether or not to use "people-first language" came up. After venting against it in editorial mode, the idea for this story broke upon me and I wrote it in a flash.

Unbeknownst to Johnny, he had woken up in a new world, the People First world. His day progressed as usual until he arrived at the Vocational Center for People Who Are Blind and Visually Impaired. He was early for his appointment, so he walked over to the nearby People With Blindness or Low Vision Store. He needed a new cane and it was the perfect opportunity to buy one.

Johnny took out what had become, overnight, the Communicator for People Who Are DeafBlind and told the clerk he wanted to check out the canes.

The clerk typed back, "Yes, I'll be happy to show you the canes. But you're a person first. May I show you our new line of swimwear?"

Johnny shook his head vigorously as he typed, "I don't need a swimsuit. I'm here to buy a cane."

"I know, but it's store policy. We have to serve you as a person first. How about some sunscreen? You do look a little red in the face. This here'll help ya."

Johnny wasn't happy but he paid for the sunscreen and inspected the canes.

Tapping his new cane, he returned to the Vocational Center for People Who Are Blind and Visually Impaired. It was almost time.

Cherie, his vocational rehabilitation counselor, tapped his shoulder and signed in ASL. "Hi! How you? Ready come?"

Johnny smiled and stood up. "Where?"

"Room B, same before. Want guide?"

"No. Myself, thanks."

When Johnny settled in his chair, he began to discuss the technology training portion of his job plan. Cherie interrupted him, "Good, good. We will talk that later. Now, first you person. Me ask you: Your back sore?"

Johnny was puzzled. "My back? Why?"

"If sore, I can help you. I have new license massage therapy. Want me help your back feel better?"

He thought about this for a moment. "Thanks, but time not want waste. Better focus—"

"Sorry, but you yourself first person, DeafBlind second. Must meet needs what person first. Don't worry, me good massage will."

Cherie tugged at Johnny to lie facedown on the conference table. As his vocational rehabilitation counselor's strong hands worked their magic, Johnny could see in his mind's eye his prospects for the future slipping away. He was amazed at how good it felt.

I DIDN'T MARRY ANNIE SULLIVAN

My wife and I encounter the same assumption many people have about a couple like us. She is Annie Sullivan to my Helen Keller. In their imagination, I am always with my wife. I cannot take a single step without her guiding arm. She is my link to the world.

We know this is the picture in their heads because of what they say. People would approach my wife to say she is a saint. People would tell me that I'm so lucky to have a wife to cook for me, clean for me, and drive for me.

Now, my wife is the most wonderful person I know. I'm indeed lucky. One glimpse of her from when we were at Gallaudet University: She was telling her girlfriends about her new boyfriend, and they wanted to know who it was. She told them that surely they'd seen this tall, handsome, brown-haired boy from Krug Hall. They weren't sure. As she tried to help them place me by sharing more details, one of them asked her, "Do you mean that DeafBlind guy?" "Yes!" "Oh! Why didn't you say so?" "I forgot."

Back to the reasons people think I'm lucky: The truth is that I do half of the cooking for our family of five. Also, I am a neatness fanatic—for me, cleaning is like breathing. The men in my family have never been strangers in the kitchen and they don't consider it unmanly to kneel and scrub the floor. I have simply followed their example, and being DeafBlind is no reason not to.

And what about driving? Yes, my wife drives the car when we pile in. But she rarely ever drives *for* me. It's just our family going out together, or us two on a date. When it's a board meeting I need to attend, or a presentation I'm giving, or a literary event to meet up with some of my writer friends—things that are for me and not for her or our boys—I take care of my own transportation.

Sometimes my "driving" myself places takes the form of a city bus, or a paratransit van, or a taxicab. More often, though, I employ an accessibility assistant, who picks me up and gives me all sorts of visual information as I do my errands. Sometimes, even when it's an event that my family is attending together,

I have my assistant there so I can participate fully without having my wife think or process things for two.

It has long been my policy, whenever we relocate and are looking for a place, to ask myself, "If I lived here alone, would I be all right? Would I be independent and be able to get around, shop, and socialize in my community?" If the answer is no—because there is no transportation access or there are no DeafBlind services—then we need to look elsewhere. My asking that question doesn't mean I'm ignoring the essence of marriage, family, or community, which is interdependence. No one is truly independent. However, there is such a thing as unhealthy dependence.

Unfortunately, some DeafBlind people are stuck in situations where their dependence on partners or family members puts them at risk. Society should be responsible for ensuring that they have the same resources, rights, and accommodations that hearing and sighted people enjoy, but this doesn't always happen. This can complicate the lives of DeafBlind people, including their relationships with others, especially significant others.

I was blessed to have many DeafBlind guides in the matter of marriage and interdependence. One was Robert J. Smithdas, who wrote in his first memoir about becoming engaged to a hearing-sighted woman. Many of his friends praised her and told him that she was perfect for him—she was generous, attentive, and so helpful! Bob was mixed up at first, because he did want to get married, badly. As the wedding date approached, however, he realized that the relationship was wrong. He dropped the engagement. He wasn't able to fully articulate why, but reading his book, I understood. He wanted a wife, not a helper. He wanted to be a husband, not a charity case.

Bob would later fall in love with a DeafBlind woman whom he had met for the first time by literally bumping into her. Talk about love at first contact! But when they tied the knot, the media unfairly made them into a "Believe It or Not!" exhibition—even *National Enquirer* ran the story. Few appreciated how sensible and normal the pairing was: most people, after all, do marry others with the same culture and background.

Another role model was Harry C. Anderson, the former president of the American Association of the Deaf-Blind. He and his Deaf sighted wife, Elaine, stayed at our home when

I was a teenager. They were in town for a retreat of families with DeafBlind children. Harry gave a training session on interdependence and used his and Elaine's life together as the model. He showed us that, while there were things he couldn't do with ease, he and Elaine were able to divide all of the daily chores and responsibilities equally between them. That made a simple but lasting impression on me.

Even with such positive models, my wife and I had to learn many things by trial and error. For example, some people would tell her to tell me hello. At first, she would relay their messages to me. Soon, though, we sensed that this was bad, and for most of these situations she would tell them to come over and say hello themselves. Also, I have had to say "No" a lot when people assume that, because I have a sighted wife supposedly at my disposal, I could go somewhere at the last minute, or read something in an inaccessible format, or take a videophone call. I gently but firmly steer them toward working with me by adapting to my needs.

None of this is to say that I never borrow my wife's eyes. I do. It's usually for quick fixes, not unlike her borrowing my height to reach something on a high shelf or borrowing my arms to open a jar. The point isn't to avoid helping each other or supporting each other. She tenderly nurses me when I'm sick, and it's my shoulder she turns to when she weeps. The point is to be aware of how society has placed me, as a DeafBlind person, at a great disadvantage in some situations, and to correct these problems in the right away—not by having my wife take on the burden and be the solution, but by confronting these barriers and tracing them back to where the real solutions are. My wife is a brilliant and assertive partner in that endeavor, as she is in all our other endeavors, and that's why I'm a very, very lucky man.

PRO-TACTILE: BURSTING THE BUBBLE

It's an exciting time to be DeafBlind. The single most important development in American DeafBlind history is in full swing. Called the Pro-Tactile movement, it's moving through the community like nothing has ever before.

Launched in Seattle, which has perhaps the country's most active local DeafBlind community, Pro-Tactile is difficult to describe with its many political, linguistical, and practical elements. I was going to write "innovations" instead of "elements," but it wouldn't have been accurate, for many of these ideas and techniques are old. But Jelica Nuccio, the former director of Seattle's DeafBlind Service Center, and aj granda, a free-thinking communication specialist, both DeafBlind, put all of these things together, enhancing each part as they went, and gave it a wholistic, philosophical package and the needed wallop to inspire change.

I will start by explaining what is—or, to put it in the past tense, *was*—the core problem in communication between DeafBlind individuals and their hearing or sighted peers. Pro-Tactile resolves this problem as well as many other issues. DeafBlind people have typically been in a bubble when communicating with others. Let's take a look at a page from Wally Thomas's 1960 memoir, *Life in My Hands*. He was deafened and blinded during World War II while serving on Great Britain's Bomb Disposal Unit. After he accidentally exploded a clump of T.N.T., he underwent a whirlwind series of surgeries. About one of these experiences, he wrote:

> During a lucid period I was told I was going to have an operation. I felt pretty good that day. I said: "What is it to be this time, a boy or a girl?" No one laughed. Some people don't appreciate a brilliant sense of humor. They just stuck a needle in my arm.

Later, after he woke up and asked for water, they wrote on his hand, "You had your operation four hours ago and the triplets are doing fine." It turned out they did appreciate Thomas's wit, but they didn't have a way to let him know or they did not think to let him know. When hearing and sighted people laugh, they assume this fact is conveyed to everyone in their presence. The needle that went into Thomas's arm didn't burst the communication bubble he found himself in. He was able to tell jokes but not know immediately if others were laughing. Others could penetrate the bubble to communicate with him, but as soon as it was Thomas's turn, he was in the bubble again, talking into empty air for all he knew. For the rest of his active life—he traveled much, wrote, and was the subject of two popular songs—most of his interactions with others were lopsided, not equally two-way. He would always miss a lot of feedback and could only trust or imagine that others were listening and reacting.

When I started listening to ASL tactilely in high school, I found it liberating. I had been relying on my increasingly blind eyes, and the turn to tactile communication was like a breath of fresh air, for I gained much more reliable information. Best of all, others proved to be happy to communicate with me in this way, whereas they had been confused or annoyed by my older requirements related to lighting, distance, signing space, color of clothes, lighting, and background contrasts.

As wonderful as it was to make this change, new problems emerged. While I was signing, all sorts of important things could be transpiring. The person with whom I was talking might suddenly look away because someone waved for her attention from across the room. I would still be signing, as if nothing had happened. If she nodded, I didn't know that. If she laughed, I didn't know until I finished my joke and it was her turn, whereupon she might say, "Ha ha." I would often ask yes-or-no questions, seeking some kind of feedback to help me proceed, only to have this be mistaken for her turn. Or, if I snatched my hand back to continue, she would feel I had been rude.

Thus, many of my conversations with sighted people resembled TTY conversations, where one person types one message at a time before typing "GA," short for "go ahead," to indicate that it was the other party's turn to type. Such conversations don't have the same dynamic flow of information, feedback, and instant cues that sighted and hearing people enjoy when talking with each other, whether in ASL or spoken English.

Also, the feeling that I was signing to the wall meant I often felt my native expressiveness fall flat. If you don't have feedback from your audience, it's hard to continue in a spirited manner. This problem sometimes made it hard for me to give a presentation. I knew I had an audience, most likely an appreciative one, but I could not feed off its energy. If I was lucky, I would have enough inner vitality to carry the presentation anyway. But not always.

Whenever I talked with fellow tactile listeners, however, I felt alive. It was always a joy to feel their hands on mine and to feel their every reaction. Our conversations flowed with electricity, and we often talked at once, whole words and phrases overlapping and chasing one after another. I felt at my most authentic, at my most eloquent.

What hadn't occurred to me but did to Jelica Nuccio and aj granda was to ask that everyone, sighted or hearing, to enter and stay in this tactile space whenever they talk with DeafBlind people. To banish forever the bubble that used to separate DeafBlind people from the people they talked to. That is what Pro-Tactile is all about. It gives everyone the tools and principles to create and maintain such tactile spaces, where DeafBlind people would enjoy equal access to information and participate fully.

When hearing people want to socialize with Deaf people, they have to become a little Deaf themselves, by using ASL, by listening visually, by giving visual cues. Otherwise, Deaf people wouldn't have equal access. This is widely understood and practiced. So the expectation that hearing and sighted people become a little DeafBlind themselves, by employing Pro-Tactile (PT) skills, shouldn't come to anyone as a shock. It's an old principle; it just hadn't been applied to the DeafBlind community until Pro-Tactile put the need for tactile access at the heart of a movement to radically improve the quality of life and social experience of all DeafBlind people.

Allow me now to touch on four practical PT communication tools: backchanneling, back-backchanneling, mapping, and the somewhat misleading heading, "Tactile ASL."

Backchanneling is the most important tool for maintaining

tactile contact. When a DeafBlind person is talking to you, you want to place a hand on her arm, shoulder, knee, or place your foot on her foot, depending on what position is easiest at the moment. If you two are standing, it wouldn't do for you to lean over so your hand is on her knee. One of her arms would serve better. But if you two are sitting at lunch, knee to knee, her knee would probably be the easiest place to register your feedback. Whatever the location, there are all kinds of signals you can give while you're listening and reacting—signals that indicate you're nodding, smiling, laughing, puzzled, shocked, wanting to interrupt, and so on. The default is simply resting your hand, which indicates you're listening but either quiet or being "silent." Breaking off this tactile contact means you're no longer listening, although it is of course better to signal "hold on" or to tell the person that your cell phone is ringing or that a friend just arrived and you want to give him a hug. The point is that tactile contact, for PT users, is now taken for granted, meaning any break in tactile contact is equivalent to a break in the communication event.

Pro-Tactile etiquette also calls for a sighted person listening in on a conversation between two DeafBlind people to place a hand on each person's shoulder to let them know she's listening in. She also gives both her reactions to their conversation, such as laughing at something one of them said. Both DeafBlind people would know this and they are given opportunities they never enjoyed before learning PT. One now has the choice of turning to the sighted listener and demanding, "You think that was funny?" or to include that person into the conversation by telling the other DeafBlind person, "Did you know that the same thing happened to her last week?" The sighted listener, now included, can sign, per one of Pro-Tactile's coolest features, sign with both hands so to give both DeafBlind listeners the same comment: "Oh yes. We really need to get those steps fixed! You're not the only ones having problems with them!"

One of the oldest techniques that Pro-Tactile builds on is the three-way tactile conversation. In such an arrangement, all three signers sign with both hands functioning as dominant hands, sometimes repeating the same two-hand ASL word twice, once for the benefit of one listener and again for the other, such as "name" and "from." "His name name what John Lee Clark, short

JLC, from from Minn." But before PT came along, the whole package, those participating in such three-way conversations did not give each other their feedback as consistently while listening. With backchanneling added, these conversations work much more elegantly.

For DeafBlind presenters, or for anyone addressing a group, there is "back-backchanneling." For many years, DeafBlind presenters have used various methods to try and connect with their audiences. One was to stop frequently to ask a question, to which the audience's overall response, such as "yes" or "no," would give the presenter a sense of connection. A community leader from Wisconsin named Ruth Silver, before learning PT, would have an interpreter sign "yes," "no," or "applause," on her arm. She told me that, even after many years using this technique, it still startled her sometimes when the interpreter gave her such audience feedback. It hadn't occurred to her to ask the interpreter to maintain continuous tactile contact, which removes this problem because it's not a momentary signal through the wall of the bubble but a stream of signals, including a default back-backchanneling signal that means the audience is quietly attentive. This signal on the DeafBlind presenter's back changes only when an arm is raised, or someone in the audience has a puzzled expression, or someone is nodding or the whole audience is nodding, or there's laughter, smiling, weeping, sighing, shock, yawning. People entering or leaving the room can no longer do so without a PT-using DeafBlind presenter knowing it instantly.

Why on the back and not just the presenter's arm? Because backchanneling is a more sophisticated art than that. The back becomes a map of the room. If a DeafBlind professor is teaching a class of students sitting in a half circle, an imaginary half circle exists on the back, and the PT back-backchanneling feeder can point to various locations in relation to this and the professor would know instantly that a student on the right has raised his arm, or another on the left has a puzzled expression, or that two in the back are yawning or looking at their smartphones. Some, upon learning of this technique, have asked me if I am ever overwhelmed by all that information at the same time I'm presenting. My answer is no. Keep in mind that hearing and sighted people get a whole lot more information, all the time, so much detail—such as the colors of students' clothes, even the words written on some of their T-shirts. Before PT, I had very little information about my audiences. With back-backchanneling, I get a lot more, certainly all of the most important items, things necessary to make me an engaged presenter. But by no means is it overwhelming, although it may get a little getting used to, as with anything new in life.

Another part of Pro-Tactile is called "maps." One problem with visual ASL for DeafBlind people concerns the giving of directions or information about places and the environment. Pointing in various directions doesn't do much for a tactile listener. Where exactly is the finger pointing, and in relation to what landmarks, and at what distances? I remember eating in a restaurant with a friend and asking him where the bathroom was. He pointed to it. I took my cane and walked there, but found a row of booths. My friend had pointed in the right direction, but the way to get there is to walk around this row of booths, around the U-shaped layout of the restaurant. While my friend quickly learned to give better directions, PT's mapping technique employs a tactile listener's other, non-listening hand as a kind of drawing board. In this case, my friend would have taken my right hand and drawn a U. "Okay," he would say, "we're here,"—pointing to the precise location in relation to the U shape—"and the bathroom is there"—pointing to that location on my hand, and he would draw a line which would be my walking path. This thenar mapping is awesomely efficient, brisk, and *accurate*. Asking sighted people to map on my hand also saves me the trouble of asking them to change the way they give verbal directions; I've found that many people pick up this skill easily. Fellow DeafBlind people are champion surveyors.

Tactile ASL, or TASL, advances the concept of utilizing DeafBlind listeners' "other" hands to describe all sorts of objects and actions. TASL is mainly the tactile counterpart to visual classifiers in ASL. Those visual classifiers don't always make sense to the tactile listener. Take size, for example. How big something is supposed to be, in visual ASL, is rarely replicated physically. One mouths a certain way and shakes his hands a certain way to convey how huge a tree is. In TASL, you take my right arm, which is now our tree, and you can say that you're this tall—say, an inch tall—in relation to this tree, placing your inch-tall self at the base of my forearm. If the tree isn't that tall, the reference would be taller, maybe two or three inches against the height of my forearm. Whatever the case may be, this technique gives me a vivid tactile picture of the tree's size.

To continue with the example of my arm doubling as a tree, you could tell a story about your dog chasing a cat up a tree. Telling that story in visual ASL might not work so well, because the parts are broken into different visual panels, now the cat running, now the dog running, now the scurrying up the tree—a visual montage. I may be missing your facial expressions—the terror the cat is feeling and the dog's glee. In TASL, you can say "cat" and with your fingers convey the exact manner in which it, terrified, scurries up the tree. I can feel viscerally its terror and soon, the gleeful bounding of the dog and the exact way it paws the lower part of the tree, barking.

I have hardly covered the tip of the huge, fantastically contoured iceberg that is TASL. There is TASL poetry, like waves rolling over the shore of your palm. There are TASL puns. TASL opens the way for DeafBlind people to get precise information about their bodies and the medical procedures they're considering, so medical interpreters must learn this if they are to do their jobs. It offers the most effective way to explain things that hinge on precision and clarity. Instructors and counselors who work with DeafBlind consumers must learn all of this to give good service. To not learn and then use TASL, and PT as a whole, is to continue denying DeafBlind people access to information.

Although TASL would be the centerpiece of any case made for recognizing the way DeafBlind signers and PT users communicate as a distinct dialect of ASL, I feel it is necessary to be precise about what the term "Tactile ASL" means. It is not, in itself, a language or even a whole dialect. ASL is still the language. ASL happens to be already very tactilely accessible, and I have reason to believe it was shaped, in eighteenth-century France, with tactile as well as visual communication in mind. However, as ASL is spoken among sighted Deaf people, the text can cease, here and there, to be meaningful to tactile hands while remaining clear to visual eyes. TASL provides alternatives to those parts of the ASL text. So, to put it precisely, "Tactile ASL" is as opposed to visual ASL, not as opposed to ASL itself. It's like saying that a car is a sports car instead of a family car. Both are still cars.

For years, the term "TASL" has been used to mean various things, causing much confusion. I wrote two articles firmly stating my opinion that there's no such thing as "Tactile ASL." I was responding to some linguists who labeled the way some DeafBlind people signed as TASL because they signed differently, such as with the absence of facial expressions. They were wrong to use this label because those DeafBlind signers were not signing differently on purpose. They could not help presenting ASL differently, just as, for example, Deaf people with cerebral palsy couldn't help signing differently. Both are signing ASL—it is their intention to do so. You did not have classes on DBASL or CPASL.

But *now* there is Pro-Tactile's TASL, which is signed on purpose and which is specifically taught. However, ASL is still the language. Further developments and linguistic research will determine whether ASL plus PT practices, especially with respect to TASL, constitutes a dialect or not.

Back to Pro-Tactile, lest anyone assume it is for tactile signers only, it can benefit *all* DeafBlind people. A Deaf man with tunnel vision uses back-backchanneling while presenting to help him look immediately at a student who has raised her hand. Without this support, it would take him a while to look around and find who may have a question. Oral DeafBlind people benefit from backchanneling while conversing. Wally Thomas would have appreciated knowing that they did laugh at his joke, and it wouldn't be hard to teach family members or friends to maintain tactile contact and give feedback. Even hearing blind people could use mapping, for the English language is notoriously confusing and long-winded when it comes to directions. Deaf sighted people would enjoy TASL. DeafBlind children would thrive with this increased connectedness and acquire language and social skills much more successfully.

Pro-Tactile is most powerful, most liberating for DeafBlind people who learn and use all of its tools, but it also helps hearing and sighted people feel connected to DeafBlind people. As one dear friend told me, "I've known you for fifteen years and have always enjoyed your company. But there was always something missing or 'off.' I wasn't sure what it was. Pro-Tactile changed all of that. Now I feel so connected with you and cherish our time together all the more." That old bubble wasn't bad for just DeafBlind people; it must have bothered thousands upon thousands of family members, spouses, and friends. It has already changed some DeafBlind people so profoundly you wouldn't recognize them. "Is that really the same person? What a beautiful smile he has now!" As aj granda has explained, many DeafBlind people used to be withdrawn or frustrated and this would be for a simple reason: lack of information.

There is so much more I want to write, but let me just say that it's an exciting time to be DeafBlind. It was cool to be DeafBlind before, but now it's incredible, because we are turning toward increased connection in a world where so many people are being isolated and separated from one another and forgetting what human contact is all about. Maybe the whole world needs the Pro-Tactile movement!

ABOUT THE AUTHOR

John Lee Clark was born Deaf and became DeafBlind in adolescence. A native speaker of American Sign Language, he attended and graduated from the Minnesota State Academy for the Deaf. Shortly after leaving Gallaudet University, he and his wife, the artist Adrean Clark, founded The Tactile Mind Press. They ran it for seven years, publishing a magazine, books, an e-zine, and works of ASL literature (via DVDs).

In 2008, Clark published a chapbook of poems called *Suddenly Slow*. The following year saw the publication of his acclaimed anthology, *Deaf American Poetry*, and a few years later, his anthology *Deaf Lit Extravaganza* appeared. For his poetry, he was featured at the Deaf Way II International Cultural Arts Festival and won grants and fellowships from VSA Minnesota, Minnesota State Arts Board, Intermedia Arts Center, and The Loft Literary Center.

Clark currently works as a Braille instructor. He enjoys spending time with his wife and three sons, tandem cycling, and surprising ladies in yarn stores when he buys supplies for his knitting projects. He is also always writing, so stay tuned for is next book!

ABOUT THE PUBLISHER

Handtype Press is a company that showcases the finest literature created by signers, Deaf and hearing alike, or about the Deaf or signing experience the world over. Our titles include John Lee Clark's anthology *Deaf Lit Extravaganza*, Kristen Ringman's Lambda Literary Award finalist *Makara: A Novel*, and Raymond Luczak's *From Heart into Art: Interviews with Deaf and Hard of Hearing Artists and Their Allies*. Handtype Press can be found online at handtype.com.

CPSIA information can be obtained
at www.ICGtesting.com
Printed in the USA
BVHW070956200220
572816BV00006B/542

9 781941 960004